PUFFIN BOOKS

UK | USA | Canada | Ireland | Australia
India | New Zealand | South Africa

Puffin Books is part of the Penguin Random House group of companies whose addresses can be found at global.penguinrandomhouse.com.

www.penguin.co.uk   www.puffin.co.uk   www.ladybird.co.uk

Penguin Random House UK

First published 2023

003

Text copyright © Roxie Nafousi, 2023
Illustrations by Arabella Jones
Stock images © Adobe Stock, 2023

The moral right of the author and illustrator has been asserted

All third-party website links are included for information purposes only and the author and publisher accept no responsibility for, and do not control, approve or endorse, any information or material contained on such third-party websites or social media platforms.

Set in 11/16pt Amasis MT Pro
Typeset by Jouve (UK), Milton Keynes
Printed and bound in Great Britain by Clays Ltd, Elcograf S.p.A.

The authorized representative in the EEA is Penguin Random House Ireland, Morrison Chambers, 32 Nassau Street, Dublin D02 YH68

A CIP catalogue record for this book is available from the British Library

ISBN: 978–0–241–65776–8

All correspondence to:
Puffin Books
Penguin Random House Children's
One Embassy Gardens, 8 Viaduct Gardens, London SW11 7BW

MIX
Paper | Supporting responsible forestry
FSC® C018179

Penguin Random House is committed to a sustainable future for our business, our readers and our planet. This book is made from Forest Stewardship Council® certified paper.

MANIFEST
for kids!

ROXIE NAFOUSI

PUFFIN

To Suraya, Sienna, Serena, Syrus, Rowena, Zachary, Sofia and Adam.

I am so lucky to be your aunty and watch you all grow up into the incredible humans that you are. Thank you for being the best cousins to Wolfe too. I love you all very much!

CONTENTS

Introduction — vii

PART ONE: FOUR STEPS TO MANIFESTING — 1

Step One: Understanding Our Emotions — 3
Emotion One: Fear — 9
Emotion Two: Worry — 19
Emotion Three: Guilt — 32
Emotion Four: Embarrassment — 40
Emotion Five: Anger — 47
Emotion Six: Sadness — 55
Looking After Ourselves — 63

Step Two: Confidence and Self-Belief — 69
There is Only One You! — 72
Accept Other People's Uniqueness — 78
Speak to Yourself Kindly — 79
Be Yourself — 84
Do What Makes You Happy — 85
Be Kind to Others Too — 88
Be Proud of Yourself — 90

Step Three: Gratitude — 93
Focus on What You Have, Not What You Don't Have — 97
Replace Moaning with Gratitude — 98

Say 'Thank You' – *Lots*!	101
Comparing Ourselves to Other People	103
Social Media	105
Step Four: Goal-Setting	109
Set Your Goals	111
Visualize Your Goals	113
Make a Plan and Take Action	115
Believe in Yourself	116
Keep Going	116
Look for Inspiration	117
PART TWO: THE JOURNAL	121
How to Use the Journal	123
Your Journal Pages	125
A Note for the Grown-Ups	239

INTRODUCTION

Hello you,

Thank you for picking up this book. I am so happy that we are going to go on this journey together!

I should probably start by introducing myself. My name is Roxie and my job is to *help people feel happier* and to *make their life the best that it can be*. The way I do that is by teaching people all over the world about something called '**manifesting**'.

> Manifesting means using the power of your mind to positively change your life.
>
> *To manifest* means *to make it happen.*

Learning to manifest can help you to:

1. **Feel happier in your life**
2. **Become the best you that you can be**
3. **Cope with challenging times**
4. **Set and reach goals**

Learning to manifest is kind of like **discovering you have a superpower.**

> **Manifesting helps you to live your best life and be whoever you want to be!**

I've used manifesting to make my whole life better. When I was younger, I didn't enjoy school very much because I never fitted in. I was often teased or left out and it made me feel really lonely. I had no confidence and I never felt 'cool'. I didn't know what to do to make myself feel better, so I stayed feeling sad for a long time. Then, when I was twenty-seven, I learned about **MANIFESTING**! This changed everything for me. Now I'm thirty-two, a mum to a little boy called Wolfe, and **I love my life**. I am confident and happy, I have a successful job and lots of amazing friends. If I could tell younger me what my life would be like now, she wouldn't believe it!

Manifesting has become my superpower, and I want to teach you how it can be yours too.

This book will teach you everything you need to know to start manifesting. I have created a **four-step guide** for you to follow, and once you finish reading, you will have all the information you need to **be the best you**. I wish I'd known this when I was at school – and I'm glad you now will!

INTRODUCTION

This book comes in two parts:

PART ONE is the **reading section**, where I'll take you through the four steps to manifesting, which include exploring our emotions, how to develop confidence and self-belief, the importance of gratitude and how to set goals. There are also exercises for you to complete throughout.

PART TWO is a **daily journal**. It will only take you a few minutes before bed each day to complete, but it will help you to put what you've learned into practice.

Keep a special pen with this book so you have it to hand when you need to fill in exercises or write in your journal.

Do you have friends reading this book too? If so, why not **try some of the exercises together**?
Or you could talk about what you've been **learning in this book** and which parts you **like the most.**

OK, shall we get started?

PART ONE
FOUR STEPS TO MANIFESTING

STEP ONE
UNDERSTANDING OUR EMOTIONS

UNDERSTANDING OUR EMOTIONS

Emotions are feelings that we experience in response to different situations. For example, we might feel happy or sad, excited or scared, angry or afraid. Every day we will feel all sorts of different emotions – and this is completely normal.

What different emotions have you felt today?
Write down as many as you can remember here:

....
....
....
....
....
....
....
....
....

Manifesting is about feeling happier and being the best you that you can be. Understanding your emotions, knowing what to do with them and letting them out in a healthy way will help you to feel better every day. It will also help you to cope better in a challenging or stressful situation.

Firstly, it is important to know that *all* emotions are valid. **It is OK to feel any kind of emotion**, whether it's excitement, sadness, worry or happiness.

Sometimes we might feel that it is 'wrong' to feel certain things. For example, we might feel that we shouldn't be angry, or that we shouldn't feel sad about something. We might hold those feelings in and try to put on a 'brave face'. **But there are no 'wrong' emotions.** We are human, which means that we will – *and are allowed to* – feel **all** the different emotions.

When we feel happy or excited, we usually find it easy to express ourselves. We might talk about it, smile, laugh, jump up and down or suddenly spring into action. (Have you ever been told you are going to a friend's house and felt so excited that within seconds you rushed to your room to pack your bag?)

It is often much simpler to express emotions that we feel are 'good'. But when we feel emotions that might be seen as 'wrong', it can be harder for us to show them. For example, if we feel sad we might try to hold back our tears, or if we feel embarrassed about something we might want to run and hide away. The problem is that when we keep our emotions locked inside us, it can actually make things worse, and it can keep us feeling that way for longer.

When we don't let our emotions out, they build up inside us. Then we can become overwhelmed and find it harder to feel happy day to day.

Nobody can feel happy **all the time,** because life always has ups and downs, good times and challenging times. **That's what makes us human!**

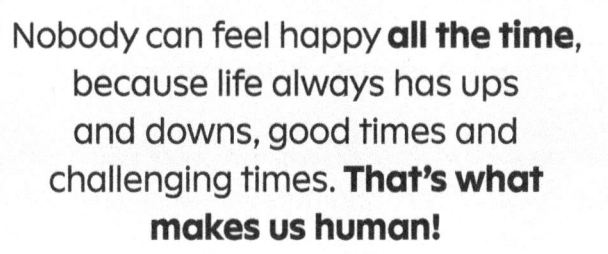

PHYSICAL SYMPTOMS

Did you know that whenever we feel an emotion, it doesn't just affect our minds but our bodies too? In fact, **our bodies often know we are feeling something before our brain has caught up**. For example, have you ever felt a funny feeling in your stomach but you didn't know why? Or have you ever noticed that your cheeks have started going red and you can't control it? Well, those things are your body reacting to an emotion like worry or embarrassment.

The changes in our bodies as a result of feeling certain emotions are called **physical symptoms.** *Physical symptoms can be used as clues to help us understand what we are feeling.*

In the first step to manifesting, I want to teach you ways to let your emotions out in a healthy way, and to give you some tools to use to help you feel better when you experience them.

The six emotions I will be helping you with are:
FEAR, WORRY, GUILT, EMBARRASSMENT, ANGER, SADNESS

For each emotion, I will give you a list of physical symptoms that might come up, and then an EMOTIONS TOOLBOX that you can use every time you feel that emotion.

You will see some of the tools mentioned more than once, because they work so well that we can use them for many different emotions.

Reading Recommendation
Take it slow, as there is a lot to learn! Perhaps start by reading one emotion a day.

EMOTION ONE: FEAR

Everybody gets scared sometimes, even people who look like they are never frightened! Fear is a natural response to something that we might feel is a threat or dangerous. The way our body reacts to fear is actually our brain's way of protecting us.

Sometimes fear is a good thing – it can keep us safe and encourage us to be careful if there is a real danger. But most of the time we feel scared even when there is no real danger or threat. For example, have you ever been scared of a shadow on the wall at night while you're trying to sleep, even though you know it's just the clothes hanging behind the door?

There are lots of different things that can make us feel scared. Here are some examples:

- Going on a big ride at a theme park
- Being alone in the dark
- Starting a new school
- Trying something for the first time
- Performing on stage
- Taking an important test

Can you think of times when you've felt scared?
Could you share them with me in the space below?

PHYSICAL SYMPTOMS

When we feel afraid, our bodies release hormones. These are substances created by our body, which influence our behaviour or mood. They put us in fight-or-flight mode. This means our body prepares us to get ready either to fight danger or to run away from the threat (even if it isn't real!). These hormones can cause changes in our bodies.

We might:

- Freeze. This is when we feel like we can't move.
- Feel sick or feel something funny in our bellies.
- Have tense muscles. Our arms or legs might feel stiff and achy.
- Have shaky legs or even feel shaky all over.
- Sweat, even though it's not hot or we're not doing any exercise.
- Feel hot and cold.
- Feel like something is stuck in our throats.

Have you experienced any of these symptoms when you were scared? Circle the ones that you remember feeling. Don't worry if you can't remember any now – next time you feel fearful maybe you can try looking out for some of them.

Sometimes we feel embarrassed if we notice any of these changes happening in our bodies, especially if we are with other people. But I want to remind you that all these reactions are *totally normal*.

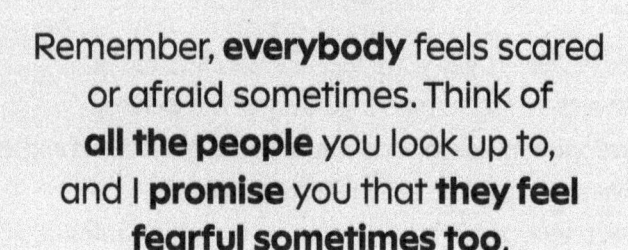

Remember, **everybody** feels scared or afraid sometimes. Think of **all the people** you look up to, and I **promise** you that **they feel fearful sometimes too**.

Don't try to 'put on a brave face' or ignore it. Instead, talk to somebody or use some of the tools I'm going to tell you about over the next few pages to help you calm down and overcome your fears! You've got this.

THE FEAR TOOLBOX

1. SAY IT

The first step in every emotion's toolbox is to SAY IT. Speaking aloud how we are feeling helps us to **validate our emotions**. Validating your emotions means you *accept and do not judge how you are feeling*. This can make us feel more in control of our emotions so that we are better able to cope with them.

> You can start by saying how you are feeling to yourself, either in your head or out loud. For example, you could say: *I am feeling scared because* . . . and then say clearly what you feel afraid of.

Next, you could talk about how you're feeling with a friend, teacher, parent or any other trusted adult. If you feel comfortable, tell them what you're thinking, and they will be able to reassure you, give you some advice or help you to feel safe.

Talking to someone about how we feel can help us feel understood. People listening to us can also make us feel cared about. So speaking about a troubling feeling can actually make you feel much better afterwards.

If we don't talk about how we feel, and we keep bottling up our feelings, we can become overwhelmed and might start to feel lonely. This can make it harder to overcome whatever you are going through.

2. BREATHING EXERCISE

As I mentioned earlier, fear can create lots of changes in our bodies. Our stomach can start doing somersaults or we may start to feel shaky and hot.

To help our bodies calm down when we're feeling some of the physical symptoms, we have to send a message to our brains to tell them that it is safe and that *the danger isn't real*. One way that we can send this message to our brain is by breathing slowly. Isn't that so clever? ***Just by breathing slowly, you can tell your brain to calm down!***

There are many exercises that help us to breathe more slowly whenever we feel overwhelmed by an emotion. I'm going to teach you a very simple one now called:

Four In, Four Out

1. Sit down or lie on your back.
2. Place one hand on your belly.
3. Breathe in deeply and slowly for four seconds through your nose. (Count to four on your fingers or inside your head.)
4. As you are breathing in, feel your belly move up and out like a balloon blowing up.

5. Exhale through your mouth for four seconds, feeling your belly go all the way back down.
6. Repeat this inhaling and exhaling for a few minutes or until you feel calmer.

Practise this now and see how it makes you feel!

3. SAY AN AFFIRMATION

An **affirmation is a positive statement** that we can say to ourselves inside our heads or out loud.

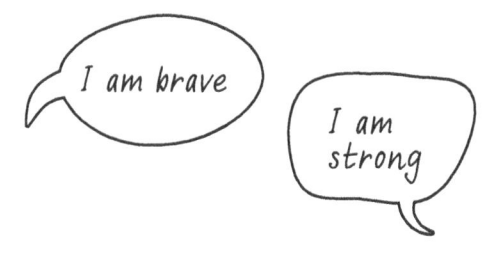

> I am brave

> I am strong

When you repeat a positive affirmation to yourself, you send good messages to your brain. This can help you to feel calmer, more confident and more in control.

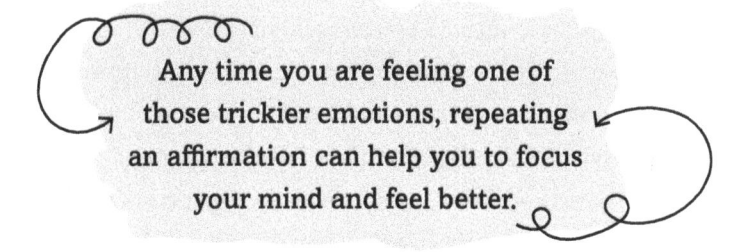

> Any time you are feeling one of those trickier emotions, repeating an affirmation can help you to focus your mind and feel better.

When you next feel afraid, try repeating these affirmations to yourself:

- *I am brave.*
- *I have nothing to be afraid of.*
- *I am safe and protected.*
- *I am stronger than my fears.*
- *I can handle anything.*

Practise repeating them to yourself now.

Even if you don't believe the affirmations as you say them, the more you say them, the more you will start to believe them – so keep practising!

4. ENCOURAGE YOURSELF

I always remember when I was playing Oliver in *Oliver Twist* at school. I was stood backstage and my legs felt like jelly. I really didn't want to go on stage because I was so afraid that I would forget my words in front of everyone. But I knew I had to do it, because otherwise I would get into trouble with my teachers, and I didn't want to let myself down either. So I became my own cheerleader. In my head I said to myself: *You can do it, Roxie. Everything is going to be OK. Just go for it!* This really helped me feel more confident. Before I knew it, I was walking on stage and **I did it**! Hooray! I felt so happy afterwards, and the next time I had to go on stage, I didn't feel so scared. Now, as a grown-up, I go on stage in front of **thousands of people** and I don't feel scared *at all*.

Has that ever happened to you before? Have you ever felt scared about doing something, and then after you have done it realized it wasn't that bad? And then the next time you did it, it felt easier and a lot less scary?

Sometimes when we feel scared our mind might be filled with ideas or worries about what might happen. But **when we encourage ourselves, we start to feel braver**. Doing this helps us face the things we are scared of, and as a result we overcome our fears and show ourselves how strong we really are!

If you find it difficult to think of what to say to yourself in these situations, imagine what you would say to your best friend if they were scared, and then say it to yourself. **Sometimes you just have to talk yourself into GOING FOR IT!**

Do you remember what tools we have inside our FEAR toolbox?

Write them down.

THE FEAR TOOLBOX

1. ....
2. ....
3. ....
4. ....

EMOTION TWO: WORRY

As you grow up, you might find you start worrying about things a little more. This is a natural part of life. Sometimes we might worry about things that are happening at home, or about our homework or an exam we have coming up. We might also feel worried if we hear people talking about something on the news that seems scary.

Sometimes we also feel worried about things that might happen in the future, or about things that haven't happened yet. This happens to me sometimes: I might worry about small things, like being late for an important meeting, or at other times I might worry about bigger things, such as getting sick or falling out with a friend.

When we feel worried about something, it can be hard to think about anything else. Worries can become overwhelming and sometimes it can feel like we are carrying them around with us everywhere we go.

There are lots of things we might worry about. Here are some examples:

- Getting the results of your homework or test
- If you think a friend is upset with you
- Not fitting in at school
- Being late
- Forgetting to pack the right things for school

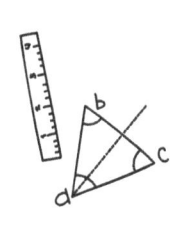

What are some of the things you worry about?
Share them with me below.

Worry can be really tricky to cope with. But remember that **worry is just a feeling**. That means that we can take control of it and find ways to let it out, overcome it and *feel better*!

PHYSICAL SYMPTOMS

When we start to worry, our bodies might start to react in the following ways:

- Heart starts racing
- Sweaty palms
- Feeling sick or getting butterflies
- Trouble sleeping
- Feeling restless and can't stay still

Have you noticed any of these things happen to you when you've been worrying about something? Circle any that you can remember!

THE WORRY TOOLBOX

1. SAY IT

First, remember that it is OK to feel worried. We *all* get worried about all sorts of different things.

Start to let your worries go by getting clear on what you are worried about. Say to yourself:

> *I am feeling worried because...*

Then **find somebody to talk to about your worries!** Sometimes we might think that we should keep our worries to ourselves or try to deal with them on our own, but this only makes us feel *worse*.

Remember: no matter what you are going through, you never need to deal with it alone!

Here are a few reasons why it is so helpful to speak about your worries with someone:

1. It will help you **feel comforted** because you will be supported and listened to.
2. The person you tell might have gone through something similar, and hearing that other people go through similar things makes us **feel less alone**.
3. They might help you **find a solution** to your problem or give you some helpful advice.

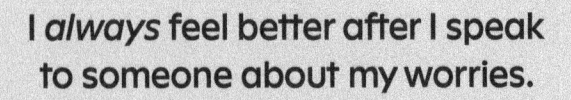

I *always* feel better after I speak
to someone about my worries.

There is a great saying:
'A problem shared is a problem halved.'
It means that when you share
a worry with someone else,
it immediately becomes smaller.

2. BREATHING EXERCISE

When we are worried, our minds can become filled with thoughts. We might feel distracted and find it hard to sit still or pay attention. Breathing exercises help us cope with worry because they **help us to focus**. When we concentrate on our breathing and pay attention to inhaling and exhaling, our minds automatically stop thinking about our worries.

There is another breathing exercise for you on the following page. Try this the next time you feel worried.

Snake Breathing

1. Sit with your back straight and make sure both your feet are planted firmly on the ground.
2. Inhale slowly through your nose for three seconds (counting inside your head or on your fingers).
3. Hold your breath for two seconds.
4. With your lips slightly open, exhale slowly through your mouth making a hissing sound like a snake!
5. Repeat for a few minutes or until you start to feel better.

Try it now and see how it makes you feel!

When we worry about something that might happen in the future, it is extremely helpful to focus instead on what is happening *right now*. Breathing exercises help us to do this because we have to concentrate on counting while we inhale and exhale, meaning we don't even have time to think about our worries!

3. CHANGE THE CHANNEL

Imagine your thoughts are like a TV. Sometimes we get stuck on a channel that is playing all our worries, *making us see bad things happening in the future*. Watching it doesn't make us feel good. Well, did you know **you have the power to choose what you think about**?

You can **change** the channel.

Imagine that you have a remote control and that you can change what you are watching. On this new channel you can watch a show that is playing happier and more positive outcomes. Watching this new channel will make you feel so much better.

Here is an example of how you could use this technique. Let's say you are worried about getting told off by your teacher for not remembering your sports kit. You are stuck on the 'worry' channel, seeing her telling you off in front of everyone. Then imagine yourself picking up a remote and switching the channel. On this new channel you could watch yourself going into your class with your sports kit *because you remembered to take it*. Or you might even see yourself speaking to your teacher and her being *understanding and kind* about you forgetting it at home.

So next time you feel worried, think about changing the channel. **Choose to imagine a better outcome** or everything working out for the best – use the power of your mind to help you feel better!

4. CHALLENGE THE WORRY

Our worries are often not based on facts and we must not let them control us. This is especially true when we are worried about what might happen in the future – we cannot predict the future, and almost all the things we worry about never actually happen!

We need to stand up to our worries and challenge them by asking them questions.

Here are some questions you could ask yourself when you're worried about something:

- *Do I know this worry is definitely true or going to happen?*
- *Have I worried about this before? What happened then?*
- *Is there a different way of looking at it or another explanation for it?*
- *What can I do to help the situation in case it does actually happen?*

For example, if a friend of mine doesn't text me back, I sometimes worry that she doesn't like me any more. So I always challenge the worry. Here's how I do it:

The worry: my friend doesn't like me any more

☹ *Do I know this worry **is definitely** going to happen or is true?*
☺ **No, I don't know for sure because she hasn't said this to me.**

☹ *Have I worried about this before? What happened then?*
☺ **Yes, I worried another friend didn't like me because I thought she was being off with me one day, but it turned out that she was just feeling a bit worried about her exams and so was focusing more on revising.**

☹ *Is there a different way of looking at it or another explanation for it?*
☺ **Perhaps she is busy or is upset about something else that has nothing to do with me.**

☹ *What can I do to help the situation if my worry is true?*
☺ **I would talk to her about it and try to make up with her.**

Next time you're worried, try answering these questions to help you to challenge and stand up to your worries. You can come back to this book to help you remember the questions. After a few tries, you will be able to remember the questions straight away and you'll become so good at challenging your worries!

5. FIND A SOLUTION

We can start to take control of some of our worries by **finding solutions.** Taking control of our worries helps us feel better because we feel more prepared and able to handle them. For example, if we are worried about forgetting to take something into school the next day, we could put it by the front door the night before to help us remember. Or if we are worried about something we hear on the news, we could ask a grown-up to explain it to us so we can understand it better.

We could also come up with a plan to help us prepare in case the thing we are worried about *does* happen. I do this a lot! For example, if I am worried about being late for an important meeting, I might test out the journey the day before to help me prepare, so I know exactly how much time I will need on the day.

Talking to another person can also help with this, as they might have ideas to help us.

Turn the page to discover my favourite tool to use when I get worried – I hope you love it too!

STRESS

When we are worrying about a lot of things at once we can start to feel *stressed*. This might happen when we feel like we have a lot of pressure on us, for example before exams or if things at home are challenging or we feel like we don't have enough time to get everything done.

When we are stressed, our body releases a 'stress hormone'. This can affect us in different ways:

- Makes us feel irritable or short-tempered
- Makes it hard to sleep
- Affects how we digest food
- Makes us feel teary or overly sensitive

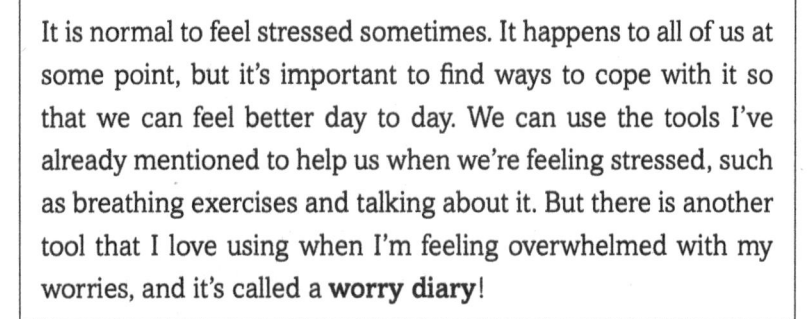

It is normal to feel stressed sometimes. It happens to all of us at some point, but it's important to find ways to cope with it so that we can feel better day to day. We can use the tools I've already mentioned to help us when we're feeling stressed, such as breathing exercises and talking about it. But there is another tool that I love using when I'm feeling overwhelmed with my worries, and it's called a **worry diary**!

6. A WORRY DIARY

When we are stressed, all our thoughts can feel tangled and messy, and this can make it harder for us to deal with them. When we keep them in our heads, the pressure can build and we can start to feel really tense, like a bottle that's been shaken up and is about to burst.

Writing things down **helps us see our worries more clearly and let them out**. *This immediately helps to take the pressure off.*

When we see our worries or problems more clearly, it's easier to find solutions for them or to *be able to challenge them.* Here is how to keep a worry diary:

1. Before bed, write down all the worries you've had throughout the day. Imagine that you are dumping them all on to the piece of paper so that you can let them go before you sleep.

2. Look at your worries and see which ones you can find a solution for and which you need to challenge.

3. When you've finished, take a deep breath and say out loud, 'I am letting my worries go.' Saying this to yourself will help you feel calmer.

4. Close the book and put it away!

5. Look for patterns in your worries.

One big benefit of a worry diary is that it can help you see patterns in your worries. *A pattern is when you see the same thing over and over again.* When you read back through your worry diary you might notice that you often worry about the same thing or worry more on the same day of the week.

It's helpful when we can spot patterns like this because it means we can prepare ourselves. For example, if you know that you always get worried the night before you have a maths class, you could use one of the worry tools the day before you have maths, *before* you start to feel overwhelmed.

If you are struggling to find any patterns, it might be helpful to ask a grown-up to look through your worry diary with you (but only if you feel comfortable doing so).

What are the six tools you can use
when you next feel worried?

Write them down.

THE WORRY TOOLBOX

1. ....
2. ....
3. ....
4. ....
5. ....
6. ....

EMOTION THREE: GUILT

Guilt is when you feel bad about something you have done. Feeling guilty about something can feel *really horrible*. It can make us think we are a bad person for doing something wrong, even if it was a mistake. This feeling can be hard to shake off.

Of course it's important to take responsibility for our actions and learn from our mistakes, **but doing something wrong does not make you a bad person**!

> We all do things that make us feel guilty sometimes, and **it is normal to make mistakes**.

When I was about six, a friend of mine at school taught me a phrase that she said I should say to my sister the next time she upset me. I didn't know what it meant, but that weekend, when my sister wouldn't share her game with me, I said it to her. My sister started crying and ran away from me. I knew I must have said something really, really mean. I felt so bad about what I had said that for weeks afterwards I had a funny feeling inside me that made me feel upset and angry with myself. I was feeling *guilty* about what I had done and I didn't know how to make that feeling go away. *I wish I'd had the guilt toolbox to help me then.*

Here are some other examples of when you might feel guilty:

- If you lied to someone about something
- If you said something that upset another person
- If you broke something, even if it was an accident
- If you took the last ice cream from the freezer when you knew someone else would want it

Can you think of some times when you have felt guilty? Share them with me below.

....

....

....

....

....

....

....

....

....

....

PHYSICAL SYMPTOMS

Here are some of the things our bodies might do when we feel guilty:

- Have difficulty sleeping at night
- Have a funny feeling in our stomach
- Our chest might feel tight
- Our muscles could feel sore
- Tiredness
- We might start slumping or slouching a lot

Have you noticed any of these things happen to you when you've been feeling guilty about something? Circle any that you can remember!

UNDERSTANDING OUR EMOTIONS

THE GUILT TOOLBOX

Here are some tools for you to use next time you feel guilty about something.

1. SAY IT

<u>Owning up to what we have done is the first step to making things right again.</u>

When you've done something that you feel guilty about, start by saying it to yourself or writing it down in a journal. For example, you can say:

> I feel really bad for lying to my teacher today.

> I felt guilty when I made an unkind joke about my friend.

Next, talk about it to somebody that you trust. You could tell a grown-up about what happened so they can give you some advice, listen to you or just remind you that you are loved.

Sometimes we worry about getting into trouble if we talk to someone about something we feel guilty about, so you could start by saying:

> I want to talk to you about something I have done that I am feeling bad about, and I would really like you to listen without getting angry with me.

I know it can be difficult to admit when we have done something wrong, but I promise you that just talking about it does help you feel better.

2. TAKE RESPONSIBILITY AND APOLOGIZE

It is important to take responsibility for our actions, rather than just holding in the guilty feeling and trying to forget about it. **Taking responsibility means owning up to what you have done and apologizing** to anybody that your actions might have affected.

When we've done something that has hurt somebody else, saying sorry helps us to mend the relationship and make things right. For example, after what happened with my sister, I should have gone to her room and said, 'What I said was hurtful and I am really sorry. I didn't mean it and I will never say it again.' If I had done that, I wouldn't have felt guilty for so long, and she would have felt better too.

I know it can feel challenging to do this, but taking responsibility and saying sorry is a key skill to learn. **It is also a very brave and courageous thing to do.** If you own up to doing something, people won't judge you for it – they will actually *respect* you!

Write an apology

Sometimes saying sorry face to face feels too hard. Instead, you could try writing a letter. Explain why or how the thing happened, then apologize and let them know you'll make sure it doesn't happen again. This is a kind gesture that will make you *and* the other person feel better!

3. LEARN FROM IT

Learning from our mistakes and experiences means that we don't keep doing the same thing over and over again. And **learning helps us to grow into the best version of ourselves that we can be**!

One thing we need to learn is *why* we did something. Did we behave in a way that is unkind because we were feeling upset or angry? We also need to *learn what we can do differently in the future* to stop it from happening again.

Next time you feel guilty about something, ask yourself these questions to help you learn from the experience:

- *Why did it happen or what led to it?*
- *Was I feeling upset or angry about something else at the time?*
- *What were the consequences of my actions? For example, did it hurt somebody else?*
- *What could I do differently next time?*

When you have learned something from what happened, *it means that you have used the experience to help you be better in the future.* You should be proud of yourself for that.

4. FORGIVE YOURSELF

Once you have owned up to what you've done, apologized and learned from it, you should then **forgive yourself**. Be kind to yourself and move forward! *Remember,* **you are still a good person** *even if you did something wrong!*

Can you remember what is in
the GUILT toolbox?

Write down the answers.

◦ THE GUILT TOOLBOX ◦

1. ....
2. ....
3. ....
4. ....

EMOTION FOUR: EMBARRASSMENT

Once I was late for assembly while the whole school was sat down quietly listening to the headmaster speak. As I was walking to find my seat I tripped and fell over in front of *everyone*! I wanted the ground to swallow me up. I felt *so embarrassed*! Another time, a boy made a joke about my new haircut in front of the whole class during maths and I was so embarrassed that I didn't want to go to school the next day. *I really needed my embarrassment toolbox then!*

> Feeling embarrassed can make us feel self-conscious and uncomfortable. It's not a nice experience at all, but I want you to remember that everybody does or says silly things sometimes, and we all have moments where we feel this way.

Here are some other examples of times that we might feel embarrassed.

- Getting the answer wrong in class
- Falling over in front of people
- Saying you like something and someone else saying it is 'babyish'
- Mixing up or forgetting your words

Can you think of times when you have felt embarrassed?
Share them with me below.

PHYSICAL SYMPTOMS

When we get embarrassed, our body can react straight away. Here are some of the physical symptoms that might come up when we feel this emotion:

- Red or flushed cheeks
- Stumbling over your words
- Sweating or feeling hot
- Shaky hands
- Heart beating quickly
- Crying
- Wanting to run away

Do you remember if any of these things happened to you when you felt embarrassed? Circle any that you can remember!

Sometimes we feel self-conscious *just because of the physical symptoms*. For example, if your cheeks start going red you might feel more embarrassed. But please know that it is a natural way for your body to respond to certain emotions.

THE EMBARRASSMENT TOOLBOX

1. SAY IT

When something happens that makes us feel embarrassed, we might try to pretend it never happened and ignore it. *But our brains don't really work like that.* Our brains store our memories, and if we don't let out the embarrassment and manage it at the time, it might come up again later!

So, as with every emotion, letting it out by saying it is the best place to start. Say to yourself:

> *I feel really embarrassed because ...*

Or you could write about it in your journal at the end of the day:

Today I felt embarrassed when ...

Sometimes you might not want to talk about it if something embarrassing happened, but *telling someone will make you feel better.* They might tell you about a time something embarrassing happened to them, which will make you feel less alone because you will see that embarrassing things happen to everyone, not just you! Or they might help you to **laugh about it together**, which is also a great way to feel better about what happened!

If someone is often making you feel embarrassed, or they are saying mean things to upset you on purpose, please speak to a teacher or grown-up about it. Don't bottle it up – let someone know so they can help you.

2. BREATHING EXERCISE

When something happens that makes us feel embarrassed, we might feel our cheeks getting red, or we might feel like we want to cry or run away. *It can feel very overwhelming.* Breathing exercises can help here too!

I love to do a simple **breathing** exercise at times like this.

Flower Breathing

1. Place one hand on your belly.
2. Inhale through your nose.
3. As you feel your belly expand, imagine a flower is blooming open.
4. Exhale through your mouth.

5. As your belly goes down, imagine the flower is closing.
6. Keep repeating the steps until you start to feel calmer.

<u>Next time you get embarrassed, try this breathing exercise!</u>

3. REPEAT AN AFFIRMATION

Affirmations can also help us when we feel embarrassed.

When we feel embarrassed, we might feel self-conscious or bad about ourselves. **Repeating an affirmation can help us be kinder to ourselves** and remind us that even if we made a mistake or did something silly, we are still capable, worthy and loved.

Next time you feel embarrassed, try saying one of these affirmations to yourself:

- *I am worthy and loved.*
- *I am confident and brave.*
- *Mistakes help me to grow.*
- *It's OK to make mistakes.*
- *I am proud of who I am.*

Can you remember what tools to use
the next time you are feeling embarrassed?

Write down the answers.

❖THE EMBARRASSMENT TOOLBOX❖

1. ....
2. ....
3. ....

EMOTION FIVE: ANGER

A lot of us, including grown-ups, really struggle with knowing what to do when we feel angry. If we don't have the right toolbox, we can get extremely frustrated and might end up shouting, slamming doors or even hitting something. *Doing this is not only wrong but can also get us in big trouble.* **Has that ever happened to you?** It's definitely happened to me! I am so happy that now I have an anger toolbox to use, and I can't wait to share it with you.

Here are some examples of when we might feel angry:

- If someone is mean to us
- If someone asks us to do things that we find too difficult
- If your sports team loses an important match
- If someone is arguing in front of us
- If we don't feel like anyone is listening to us
- If a friend or sibling takes something of ours without asking

Can you share some examples of when you have felt angry?

....

....

....

....

....

PHYSICAL SYMPTOMS

When we get angry, our body can react in these ways:

- Feeling hot
- Fast, shallow breathing
- Clenching fists
- Heart racing
- Sweaty palms

Have you noticed any of these happen to you when you've got angry? Circle any you can remember.

Remember, it's normal to feel angry, but it is not OK to hit something because of it.

THE ANGER TOOLBOX

1. SAY IT

One of the trickiest things about feeling angry is *knowing how to express it in a safe and healthy way*. Often we will want to shout or scream. That's because anger usually comes from something that has made us feel upset or frustrated. For example, if somebody else has done something to hurt us or if we are finding something difficult, thinking that we will never be able to do it right.

The fact is that screaming at someone never makes us feel better. But *talking about it does*!

So first we have to **validate** our emotion by saying exactly what we are feeling. Remember, *validating our emotions means accepting how we feel and allowing it to be OK*. Say to yourself:

I am angry because . . .

The answer will help you to figure out what *exactly* is making you feel that way. You could also try writing about it in a journal.

Then find someone to talk to calmly about what it is you're feeling.

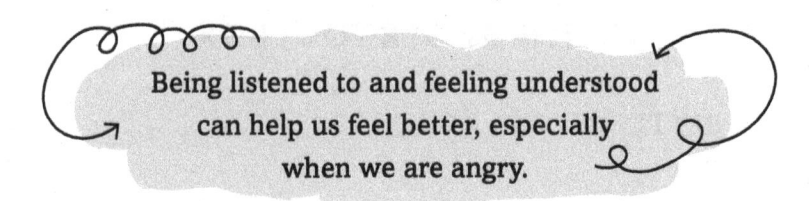

> Being listened to and feeling understood can help us feel better, especially when we are angry.

2. BREATHE

Imagine that the way you feel is measured on a thermometer and that anger is right at the top where it's piping hot. When you're really hot, it's hard to think straight and you can feel frustrated and furious. Breathing exercises help you to turn down the temperature so you feel calmer and more able to cope with the situation that caused you to feel angry in the first place.

I have shared three different breathing exercises with you already. I'd like you to think about which one is your favourite, and then choose that to be the breathing exercise you use for anger.

Just to remind you, the three different exercises are:

- **Four In, Four Out**
  Hand on belly, inhaling for four counts and exhaling for four counts (see page 14).

- **Snake Breathing**
  Inhaling through your nose, exhaling through your mouth and making a hissing sound (see page 23).

- **Flower Breathing**
  Inhaling as you imagine a flower opening and blooming, and exhaling as you imagine the flower closing (see page 44).

Circle the one you're going to use!

As soon as you notice you are beginning to feel angry, or some of those physical symptoms begin, you can use your breath to make yourself feel better straight away. Remember, by breathing slowly we send a message to our brain that tells our body to **calm down**.

3. GET PHYSICAL: *THE RIGHT WAY*

Sometimes when our anger starts to really boil up we might want to hit something to let it out. But this is not the right way to express our anger. It won't help us and it might hurt someone else too.

Instead, we can let out our anger in a much healthier and safer way by getting physical in *the right way*. You can also think of anger like **energy that we just have to use up somehow to feel better**! You could go for a run, a long walk, a bike ride or dance! My niece Sienna told me that when she is angry she loves to play on her drums because it helps her to get the anger out, and then she feels better afterwards! *Can you think of how you might like to let out your anger?*

4. COMMUNICATE

If the thing you're angry about involves another person, talking about it with them calmly is one of the best ways to deal with the situation. This is different to tool 1, 'Say It', because here you will be resolving the issue with another person, rather than only telling someone you trust about your difficult feelings.

If you aren't ready to talk calmly yet, use tool 2 or 3 (do a breathing exercise or go for a walk), and then come back to this step.

Communicating with somebody about how you feel can **help you to understand** why you're feeling angry, and it gives the other person a chance to work with you to **make things better**.

Communicating also means listening! Sometimes when I'm angry I can only see my point of view. I can become stubborn and refuse to listen to somebody else's side of things. *That keeps me feeling angry* and it can cause arguments to last longer than they should.

When I think about what the other person might be feeling, and see their side of things, *the anger just seems to go*. Instead of fighting with them, I can be kind to them, meaning that we can resolve things faster! For example, if you are having an argument with your sibling or a friend, instead of shouting at each other, you could talk about why you are both upset or frustrated, *making sure to listen to the other person*. Then you can come to a compromise or an understanding together so you can move forward.

Can you remember what is in the ANGER toolbox?

Write them down.

◆ THE ANGER TOOLBOX ◆

1. ....
2. ....
3. ....
4. ....

EMOTION SIX: SADNESS

We all get sad sometimes. We might just feel a bit down in the dumps, or we might feel really upset about something and just want to cry a lot. Feeling sad can stop us from enjoying the things we usually find fun. For example, if you're feeling sad about something that happened at school, you might feel like you don't want to see your friends that evening, even though that's something you normally love doing.

I used to feel sad a lot when I was younger, mostly because I felt so lonely. I also thought that I was the only person that ever felt sad and that made me feel *even worse*. I wish I knew what I know now.

Every single person gets sad sometimes, and **nobody is happy all the time.**

Here are some examples of things that might make us feel sad:

- If you didn't get the results you wanted in a test, even when you had worked really hard for it
- Someone in your family being poorly
- Feeling like you don't fit in
- Falling out with a friend

Can you remember a time when you've felt sad?
Share it with me below.

....
....
....
....
....
....

PHYSICAL SYMPTOMS

When we feel sad, here are some of the ways our body might respond:

- Feeling extra tired
- Slouching/hunching your shoulders
- Not feeling hungry
- Headaches
- Sore/stiff muscles

Have you noticed any of the above happening to you when you've been sad? Circle any you can remember.

THE SADNESS TOOLBOX

1. SAY IT

If we keep our sadness in, we carry it around with us like a heavy weight on our shoulders, and that can make it hard for us to feel good day to day. *It's important to find ways to cope with sadness*, so we can shake off that weight and feel like ourselves again.

When we feel sad, the **best thing** we can do is talk about it!

Start by saying to yourself:

I am feeling sad because . . .

Then **write about it in a journal**.

Writing about how you feel is an amazing way to let out your sadness, *especially if you don't yet feel ready to talk about it with somebody else*. **Your journal can be a safe space for you to let everything out.** Try starting with 'Dear Diary, today I am feeling . . .' and then write as much as you can about what you are feeling and thinking.

When you are ready, find a trusted friend or a grown-up to talk to. Remember, **a problem shared is a problem halved**. Talking to other people about what's going on can make us feel supported and comforted, and sometimes *that is all we need* to feel better!

Whenever I feel sad, I talk to my family and friends, and they always cheer me up. Sometimes they make me laugh, other times they give me a cuddle, and sometimes they just listen to me, which makes me feel cared about and loved.

2. CRY IF YOU NEED TO

Science has proven that when we cry, we feel better. So don't hold it in – let it out!

> Remember, **everyone cries** – boys and girls, old and young.

3. CHOOSE A FEEL-GOOD ACTIVITY

When you feel sad, it's easy to keep thinking about the things that are making us feel bad. So it can be helpful to distract yourself with an activity that you enjoy. Choose something that will make you smile! It could be playing football, dancing, colouring or baking a cake.

Which activities make you smile?
Write down as many as you can think of here:

....

....

....

....

....

....

....

Choose one of these activities to do the next time you feel sad!

> If you have been feeling sad for a long time, please don't keep it to yourself. Speak to a teacher or someone in your family about how you've been feeling. I promise that they can help. You are not alone!

Sometimes when we feel sad,
we might wonder when we
will ever feel happy again.
But I can tell you with certainty
that **you absolutely will**,
sooner than you think.
Sadness always passes.

Use your tools and be kind to yourself. There is always light at the end of the tunnel.

Do you remember the tools we can use to help us when we are feeling sad?

Write down three tools to remind yourself.

❖ THE SAD TOOLBOX ❖

1. ....
2. ....
3. ....

AT-HOME CHALLENGE

Every night for one week, ask each person in your family to share what different emotions they felt that day and why. It is helpful to see that we all have different feelings each day, and it is a good way to practise talking about our emotions with other people!

FINAL THOUGHTS ON EMOTIONS

Emotions are like clouds in the sky – they come and go – and they are constantly changing. When we don't know what to do with them, they can pile up like thick, stormy clouds, making things feel dark and gloomy. But when we use our toolboxes, we help them to float away and make space for the sun to shine on us again, making our day feel brighter and warmer.

> Instead of letting our emotions weigh us down, or make us feel bad about ourselves, we must learn to accept them, talk about them and find ways to let them out safely. This will help us feel happier.

LOOKING AFTER OURSELVES

Manifesting is about becoming the best you that you can be! To do this we have to **look after ourselves**. This means we must take care of our bodies **and** our minds.

*Looking after our **bodies** helps us to:*

- Feel healthier
- Have more energy

*Looking after our **minds** (our thoughts, feelings and emotions) helps us to:*

- Feel more confident
- Feel happier day to day
- Cope with challenging times

Here are some ways we can look after our minds and bodies:

- Exercise regularly and drink plenty of water
- Spend time outdoors (preferably in nature)
- Go to bed at the same time each night (and not too late!)
- Eat healthy food (like lots of different fruits and vegetables)
- Write in a journal (We'll learn how to do this in Part Two)
- Meditate (I'll teach you more about this on page 65)
- Repeat affirmations
- Practise gratitude (I'll teach you more about this later too)

Put a tick next to any you already do, and circle any that you think you could start doing!

ROUTINES

To see the real benefits of doing any of these things, we have to do them *often*. One way we can practise doing them more often is to **follow a *routine***.

I want you to make up your own routines, one for the morning and one for the evening. To do this, choose two (or more!) of the practices on page 63 to do every day. Here is an example of what a routine could look like.

MY ROUTINE

Day 1:	*Morning* *repeat affirmations, eat a healthy breakfast*
	Evening *journal, go to bed early*
Day 2:	*Morning* *affirmations, healthy breakfast*
	Evening *meditate, journal*
Day 3:	*Morning* *exercise, practice gratitude*
	Evening *journal, affirmations*

MEDITATION

Before we go to the next step, I want to talk to you about something called **meditation**.

Our minds are often very busy. Sometimes the brain is like a monkey, jumping around from one thought to the next. One minute we might be listening to what our teacher is telling us and the next we are thinking about what we want for dinner, and then our mind wanders to what our friend said to us at break time! Some people call this the **'monkey mind'**.

One way that we can look after ourselves is to give our busy minds a break – *time to rest and recharge*. Meditation helps us do this. It is **a practice that helps you to quieten that monkey mind** by encouraging it to focus on what is happening *right now* (this is also called 'the present moment'). This means you aren't thinking about what's going to happen later or what happened in the past. Instead, you are focusing on the present.

Remember, *manifesting is about living your best life*. Regularly practising meditation helps us to do that thanks to its many benefits. Some benefits of meditation are:

- It calms us down when we feel overwhelmed, stressed, sad or angry.
- It makes space in our minds to help us be more creative, come up with new ideas or problem-solve.
- It helps us sleep better and fall asleep more easily.
- It helps us with concentration (which makes this a great tool to use if you're struggling to stay focused at school!).

So how do you do it? Sometimes people meditate on the floor cross-legged. Or you can also meditate lying down on your back or sat on a chair.

Did you know that you've already practised meditating while reading this book? **In the breathing exercises I gave you in your emotion toolboxes, you were actually meditating! Breathing in and out slowly, and focusing on your breath, is one form of meditation. Well done, you!**

Here are a few other ways to meditate. Can you try one of these now?

1. **Listen to a guided meditation.** This is a great option if you are new to meditation. In a guided meditation, a voice will tell you what to do and help lead your imagination. These are easy to follow and they often play relaxing music in the background too! There are lots of guided meditations on YouTube or different apps. I have also recorded free kids' meditations for you to try, which are available from my website: www.roxienafousi.com
2. **Visualize.** Close your eyes and use your imagination to play a calming or happy scene in your mind. For example, you could play one of your favourite memories or imagine yourself in a place where you feel calm, safe and relaxed. *When we play happy scenes*

in our minds, our brains send signals to our bodies that tell it to relax!

3. **Teddy/toy meditation.** Lie down on your back. Place your favourite small teddy or toy on your belly and focus your attention on watching it move up and down as you breathe in and out slowly. Remember to inhale through your nose and exhale through your mouth as you do this. You could set a timer before you start so you know when to finish. Try three minutes first, then gradually increase the time each day. I usually like to meditate for ten minutes.

Meditating is about focusing your mind and slowing down your monkey mind! This can be tricky at first, so don't worry if you find it hard to sit still or relax. This is totally normal. It takes practice, but keep trying and over time you will find it easier and easier to slow down your mind and relax. This is a skill that will help you throughout your life!

TRY IT WITH YOUR FRIENDS

Find a time to meditate together. Perhaps you could all meditate together at break time? Each day you could challenge yourselves to do one minute longer than the day before!

STEP TWO
CONFIDENCE AND SELF-BELIEF

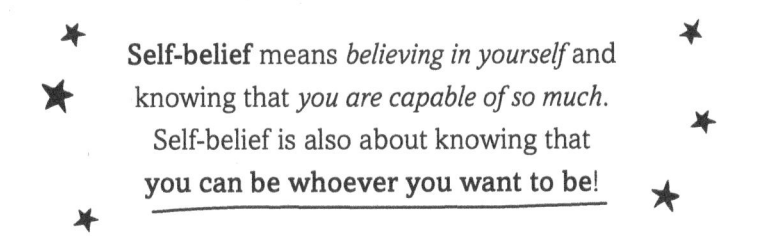

Self-belief means *believing in yourself* and knowing that *you are capable of so much*. Self-belief is also about knowing that **you can be whoever you want to be**!

Confidence is like self-belief, but it is more about *feeling sure of yourself. This feeling makes you more comfortable doing things in your day-to-day life*. For example, if you feel confident in maths, you will feel comfortable going into class. Or if you are a confident dancer, you won't feel nervous about being in the middle of the dance floor! On the other hand, if you don't feel confident, then you might feel nervous going into those situations.

Imagine that you are a tree. To be able to grow into the most magnificent tree possible, you need strong roots underground. **Self-belief and confidence are your roots**. The more confident you are, and the more you believe in yourself, the stronger your roots will be. These roots allow you to grow into the best version of yourself. They help you flourish and grow, and help you to stay strong through all seasons, even during stormy times. This is what manifesting is all about.

We need both self-belief and confidence to manifest our best lives and become our best selves. They help us to:

- Think more positively about ourselves
- Feel more motivated to do things
- Reach our goals
- Do things we might be afraid of
- Keep going when things get tough
- Feel happier
- Try hard things
- Make new friends

When I was younger, I didn't have much confidence or self-belief, and I didn't know it was something you could learn. But when I got older I started to believe in myself, and it was the best thing I ever did! *I only wish I had done it sooner.* Perhaps you also struggle with these things. I understand how that feels, but I promise you that together we can find ways to change that for the better! When we do, you will start to unlock all the power and potential within you.

THERE IS ONLY ONE YOU!

I have something very important to tell you. Read this carefully.

You are so special, exactly as you are! **Yes. YOU!**

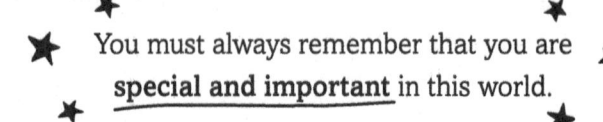

You must always remember that you are **special and important** in this world.

Do you know what makes you so special? Well, on this whole planet, with billions of people on it, there is **no one else who is the same as you**. There is only ONE you in the whole world. Isn't that cool?!

Imagine the world is like a huge jigsaw puzzle with billions of tiny pieces. Every little piece is a person.

One of those pieces is YOU, and the world needs you *exactly as you are* to fit into the puzzle and complete the beautiful picture!

CELEBRATING YOU!

I want you to celebrate all the things that make you, YOU, so I have created an **exercise** to help you see all the things that make you unique.

On the next page there is space for you to answer some questions about YOU.

I want you to write down the answers to the questions below. I've listed some possible answers for you to pick from, or you could come up with your own.

1. What words describe you?

You could choose: **kind, fun, brave, strong, independent, clever, funny, creative, responsible, honest, helpful, playful, adventurous, patient, trustworthy, imaginative and caring**

2. What are you are good at?

This could be one of your subjects at school, a hobby, being a really kind friend, remembering all the words of your favourite songs or coming up with new games to play.

3. What are some of your favourite things?

This could be your favourite colour, your favourite things to do in your free time, your favourite game or your favourite food.

4. What do you think your friends and/or family love the most about you?

If you find it hard to think of an answer, you could tell your friends or family about this exercise and ask them to help you.

Well done for completing the exercise and thank you so much for sharing your answers with me! You have just written down many of the different things that make you unique. Every single person who does this exercise will have different answers. No two people's answers will be the same because:

★ Each one of us is **different**.

Differences are what makes us **unique**.

Being unique is what makes us **one of a kind.**

Being one of a kind is what makes us **so special**.

AT-HOME CHALLENGE

It's time to teach your family how to do this exercise! Sitting together, give each person a piece of paper and ask them to draw a space for them to write down their answers, like the one on the previous page.

Ask everyone all four questions so they can fill in the page with all the things that make them unique. You can do yours again with them if you like, and you might even think of some new things to add!

CONFIDENCE AND SELF-BELIEF

When you've all finished, notice how everybody's page is different but that they are all equally wonderful.

Here is an example of one I did with my family.

WOLFE

1. Funny, brave, kind, clever, imaginative
2. Climbing, making people laugh, drawing, doing puzzles, running
3. The colour orange, cupcakes, watching Bluey, cars, playing pretend
4. That I am so much fun to be around, and I am so thoughtful and kind

WADE

1. Adventurous, creative, strong, responsible, playful
2. Acting, making up games, sports, listening to other people
3. Being in nature, dogs and all animals, watching movies
4. That I make everybody feel good when I am around

ROXIE

1. Patient, caring, clever, independent, honest
2. Writing, giving advice, reading bedtime stories, yoga
3. The colour brown, eating chips, dancing, going on long walks
4. That I am very generous and always try to help

ACCEPT OTHER PEOPLE'S UNIQUENESS!

We are all different in lots of different ways. It is important to appreciate our own uniqueness but also *other people's* as well.

Other people will do lots of things differently to you: they might like different things, speak with a different accent, be scared of different things or eat different food.

Sometimes when we see people doing something differently to us we might not understand why. But even if we don't understand, we must always **accept and be kind** about it.

> It's OK for other people to be different to us. In fact, **it's a good thing**!

Think about it like this: imagine you need to put together a football team at school. If everyone had the same skills, everyone would want to play the same position. That wouldn't be very helpful, would it? A team of goalkeepers wouldn't do very well at scoring any goals, and a team of strikers wouldn't be very good at defending! For a great team you need lots of different people who are good at different things. Or imagine an orchestra. You need all sorts of different instruments to make the music sound as beautiful and wonderful as it can be.

If somebody does something differently to you, instead of judging them or criticizing them, **try asking them questions** to help you understand them better.

I remember when I was at school, my mum would always pick me up wearing a headscarf to cover her hair. One day, a boy in my class teased me about it and I was so hurt. I wish that instead of teasing me, he had come up to me and asked me why my mum wore a headscarf. I could have explained to him that it was because of her religion, Islam, and that it is part of a tradition. Maybe this would have helped him realize that everyone is different, and that it was something he needed to accept.

Accept other people's differences, be kind and curious, and ask questions politely so that you can understand other people better!

SPEAK TO YOURSELF KINDLY

One of the best ways to feel more confident, and believe in ourselves more, is to speak to ourselves kindly.

It is very important to talk to ourselves with kindness and compassion, because our thoughts and the things we say to ourselves have a big impact on how we feel and how we behave. For example, if we say to ourselves 'I can't do this' or 'I'm rubbish at this', then we won't feel very good and we probably won't even want to try. But if we say to ourselves 'I am brave enough to try' or 'I'm going to give it my best shot', then we will feel better and braver, and are more likely to *give it a go*!

We have the power to choose how we speak to ourselves, so practise using words that help you to feel your best! **Here are positive changes you can make to the way you speak to yourself:**

Instead of saying . . .	Say . . .
I can't do it.	I am brave enough to try.
I'm no good at this.	I am doing my best and that is enough.
I wish I was better.	I get better every time I try.
What if I fail?	I'm going to give it my best shot.
I'm not as good as my friends.	I have my own strengths, but I don't have to be the best at everything.

CONFIDENCE AND SELF-BELIEF

Try to always use kind language when you talk to yourself.
Talk to yourself like you would talk to your best friend!

AFFIRMATIONS

I asked my niece Sienna when she has felt unconfident or unsure of herself. She said that sometimes when she has to sing a solo in her music class, she gets nervous because she worries that people won't like how her voice sounds.

We spoke about how, when she feels that way, she can say a positive affirmation to herself to help her feel more confident and overcome her worries. Do you remember this tool from Step One (see page 15)? Affirmations can be said inside our heads or out loud to help us focus on positive thoughts. For example, she could say to herself:

I can do it.

I am brave.

Saying affirmations can help us become more confident in any situation.

When we say affirmations often, we *train our brains* to:

1. Focus on the positives
2. Feel more confident
3. Believe in ourselves

Positive affirmations are the perfect tool for manifesting!

Here are some affirmations that you can use to improve your confidence and self-belief:

I am loved just the way I am.
I am strong.
I believe in myself.
I can be anybody I want to be.
I am proud of myself.
I deserve to be happy.
I get better every day.
I can do anything I put my mind to.
I can overcome any obstacle.
I am excited for the future.
I am enough.
I believe in myself.
I am brave and courageous.
I am special and unique.
Today is going to be an amazing day.
I am always learning and growing.
I can get through anything.
I matter to the people in my life.
I am a good person.
I can and I will.

It is enough to do my best.
I am worthy of love and happiness.
I am important to the world.
Challenges help me grow.
I am amazing.

Try saying some of these now and notice how good it feels to say them!

USE AFFIRMATIONS EVERY DAY

You can say an affirmation whenever you need a confidence boost, but you should also make them part of your daily routine and find time to say them every day. *The more you say them, the more effective they will be.*

I love saying my affirmations in the morning, at the very start of the day. If you start your day with an affirmation like 'Today is going to be an amazing day' or 'I am loved just the way I am', then your brain will try to find evidence throughout the day to support that statement. This means that your brain will make an effort to look out for positive things and help you find more reasons to feel good.

I want you to **get into a daily habit** of saying affirmations to yourself every morning. You could do this:

- As soon as you wake up, before you get out of bed
- While you are getting ready in the bathroom
- Just before you leave the house
- On the way to school

Can you go back to the routine you made for yourself earlier and add in your affirmations (see page 64)? Try to say each affirmation to yourself **five times**! Like this:

> I am loved.
> I am loved.
> I am loved.
> I am loved.
> I am loved.

BE YOURSELF

Sometimes there is a lot of pressure to be popular or cool and it can be very overwhelming. We might feel we have to change who we are or the things we like just to fit in. Have you ever felt like that?

It's normal to worry about what other people might think about us, but *manifesting is about being brave enough to be yourself.* That means that you don't try to change yourself for other people, but instead *keep celebrating, and feeling proud of all the things that make you, YOU!*

I think that the coolest people are those who aren't afraid to be different and who are proud of their uniqueness.

When you can be yourself, and you feel free to show all your unique qualities, you become *so* much more confident! When you are being yourself, you will also make friends with people who appreciate and *accept you just as you are*, and this means you will feel happier, safer and far more comfortable around those people.

It is better to have just one or two friends who love **you as you are** than lots of friends who like you for who you pretend to be.

DO WHAT MAKES YOU HAPPY

Always keep being yourself and doing the things that make you feel happy. Whether that is dressing in a certain way or choosing how you spend your free time.

What are the things that make you happy?

....
....
....
....
....
....

No matter what anyone says, you should always be proud to do these things. The things you've written down are part of who you are! And you should LOVE who you are!

Of course, the things that you enjoy doing may change as you grow up, and that's totally normal!

But you are the only one who should decide when to stop liking something or when something no longer makes you happy!

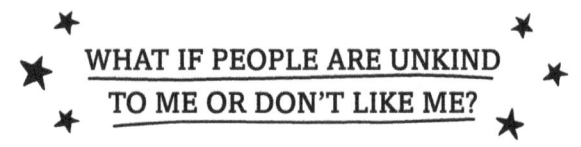

WHAT IF PEOPLE ARE UNKIND TO ME OR DON'T LIKE ME?

There are always going to be people who are unkind. These people might tease us or say things behind our backs, and I know that can feel *so horrible*. It can make us feel embarrassed or bad about ourselves. It can be especially upsetting if we feel that somebody doesn't like us when we haven't done anything to hurt or upset them. But there is something very important I need to tell you, *and I need you to really concentrate here*:

> When somebody is unkind to you for no reason, **it has absolutely nothing to do with you!**

I know that might seem hard to believe, but *I promise you it is true*. The reason they are unkind is because of how **they** are feeling. They might not be very happy or they might not like *themselves* very much, and that might make them take out their own hurt on somebody else. *If everybody could get better at dealing with tricky emotions, like we talked about in Step One, I think everyone might be a bit kinder and nicer to each other too, because then we wouldn't take our hurt out on anyone else!* Another reason why someone might be unkind to you is because they are jealous of you, and they want something that you have.

So the next time somebody isn't nice to you, remember that it's *nothing to do with you*. Instead of blaming yourself or allowing it to make you feel bad, here's what you could do:

1. **Ignore it**. Sometimes it is best just to let it go and rise above it.
2. **Stand up for yourself**. Be calm but strong. Tell the person how their actions are affecting you and let them know that it is not OK to continue doing it.
3. **Talk to a teacher or a grown-up**. They can support you and find a solution to make things better.

Another reason confidence and self-belief are so important is because when our roots are strong, we aren't so easily affected by what other people say or do to us.

BE KIND TO OTHERS TOO

Being kind to others means that we treat them the way we would like to be treated. **Kindness is cool**, and we should always be kind to ourselves *and* other people!

> Sometimes people who are feeling sad or lonely **don't want to show it.** When you are kind to people, you might be helping someone who is secretly having a really bad day.

Kindness comes in many forms. **Here are some examples of how to be kind to someone:**

1. Asking them how they are
2. Helping them if they are stuck
3. Giving them a hug if they are upset
4. Sharing your things with them
5. Teaching them something new
6. Giving them a compliment
7. Sticking up for them if someone else is being mean
8. Going to sit with them if they are sat on their own
9. Listening to them if they need someone to talk to

Can you think of times when you've been kind to someone?
Share them with me below.

....

....

....

....

....

....

....

....

....

....

....

....

My mum always used to say to me, 'It's nice to be nice.'
And she was right – it *does* feel good to be kind!

BE PROUD OF YOURSELF

Another way we can feel more confident and have more self-belief is to feel proud of ourselves. This means feeling good about the things we have done and what we are doing well.

There are so many things that we do *every day* that we should be proud of. **We might be proud that:**

- We tried something new
- We helped somebody else
- We kept going even when we felt afraid
- We did some chores around the house
- We learned something new
- We stood up for ourselves
- We finished a task

Sometimes we forget to feel proud of ourselves, especially if we put a lot of pressure on ourselves to be 'the best'. I'd like to encourage you to take the pressure off yourself to do something 'perfectly' and instead see that **any progress is worth being proud of**! For example, if you took part in a sports day race, you should feel proud of yourself no matter what position you came. *You should be proud that you showed up, proud that you tried and proud that you finished!*

We can also forget to feel proud of ourselves for the smaller things we do day to day, like making our bed or finishing our homework on time. We need to pay more attention to all the amazing things that we do, *big and small*!

Now I want you to think of all the things that you have done recently that you are proud of. If you're struggling to think of things to write down, you could ask a grown-up to help you.

....
....
....
....
....
....
....
....
....
....
....
....

Look at all the things you wrote down. That's amazing! Well done, you! I want you to say to yourself now: 'I am so proud of myself for doing all these things.'

AT-HOME CHALLENGE

Every evening for seven days, sit down with your family and ask each person to share three things they were proud of doing that day. This will help you all to pay attention to your achievements, which will make you all feel better about yourselves at the end of the day.

FINAL THOUGHTS ON CONFIDENCE AND SELF-BELIEF

You are so wonderful, special and unique. *The world needs you, just as you are.*

I want you to remember to be kind to yourself (and others), to BE YOURSELF, to celebrate your uniqueness, to repeat your affirmations and to pay attention to all the things that you can be proud of every day. This is an important step to helping you become the best version of you.

Self-belief is your superpower.
If you believe you can, you will!

STEP THREE
GRATITUDE

Manifesting is about making your life the best that it can be. To do this you need **gratitude**.

Gratitude means being thankful for what we have. It helps us to focus on all the good things in our lives and *really appreciate them.* **By appreciating and focusing on all the amazing things that we already have, we immediately feel happier.**

Feeling grateful is
kind of like magic too.
When we are thankful for all
the things we already have,
life gives us **more** things
to be thankful for!

There are *so* many things that we can be grateful for. Here are some examples.

Things in the world:

- Nature, which gives us trees to climb and oceans to swim in
- The different seasons, which give us snow to make snow-angels, and sunshine to keep us warm when we splash in the water!
- All the different animals that exist in the world

Things in your life:

- Having a bed to sleep in at night
- School, which teaches us so much every day
- Our family and friends
- Our favourite games or hobbies
- Our favourite food

Things about you:

- Our unique talents or qualities that make us who we are
- Our ability to learn new things
- Our body and what it allows us to do
- Our imagination and creativity

What are you grateful for?
Write down as many things as you can think of.

....

....

....

....

....

....

When you think about all the things you're grateful for, it can make you feel better because your brain is focusing on the positive things in your life. Sometimes if I'm having a bad day, I write a gratitude list like this to cheer me up. You should try it next time you feel down – *it really does make a difference!*

Gratitude can really help when we are going through challenging times – for example, if we are sick or if we've not received a good mark on our school work. When things feel hard, it can be easy to only think about what is going wrong, but if we can find little things to feel grateful for, it will make us realize that there are a lot more good things in our life than we might have originally thought.

FOCUS ON WHAT YOU HAVE, NOT WHAT YOU DON'T HAVE

When we don't get what we want, or when everything isn't exactly how we like it, we might start to complain or moan. We focus on what we don't have or on the *negatives*. *But moaning only makes us feel worse.*

Of course it's OK to say when we feel sad, worried, guilty or angry. *We should always feel like we can say if we're having a difficult time.* But if we spend too much time talking about the things that we don't have, or complaining about a situation, we might get stuck in feeling bad. Instead, we should try to **shift our focus on to the good things in our lives by practising gratitude.**

REPLACE MOANING WITH GRATITUDE

When you notice you want to complain about something, can you try to find something positive to say instead, even if it's something small? For example, imagine you come into the kitchen for dinner, and see you aren't going to be having the meal you were hoping for. Instead of saying, **'I didn't want to eat vegetables tonight. I only wanted burgers!'** you could say

> *I am glad I have a healthy dinner to eat today because I'm really hungry.*

Or instead of saying, **'I wish it wasn't raining today,'** you could say

> *I'm glad the plants and the grass are getting some water so the flowers can bloom and the grass can get greener.*

Remember that the things we think about and say out loud have a big impact on how we feel and how we behave. In the last chapter (see page 80), we spoke about how reframing your words to be more positive can help with your confidence and self-belief. But here are some other changes you could make to what you say, which will help you practice gratitude:

Instead of saying . . .	Say this . . .
I don't like this.	It's not my favourite, but what I do like about it is . . .
I wish I had more.	I am grateful for what I already have.
I never get what I want.	I often get what I want but not this time.
I'm bored.	I'm going to find something to do.

Whenever you notice yourself saying something negative, try to say something positive like the phrases above instead.

Moaning rarely helps you feel better, **but focusing on the good in your life** can make a world of difference!

You should also try to focus on what you can do to make a situation better. Think about how you can find a solution to the problem, rather than waiting for somebody else to make it better for you. *This is how you take responsibility.*

AT-HOME CHALLENGE: GRATITUDE JAR

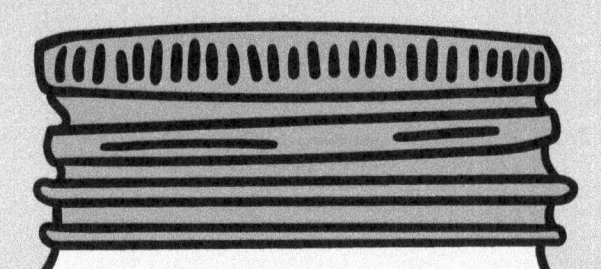

1. Find a big jar and make a label to stick on it that says 'GRATITUDE JAR'.

2. Every Friday, ask each person in your family to write down their name, the date and three things they were grateful for that week on a piece of paper.

3. Put the pieces of paper in the jar.

4. Repeat steps 2 and 3 every week until you fill the jar all the way up to the top.

5. Once it's completely filled, read out all the good things that have happened! It will feel SO good!

SAY 'THANK YOU' – *LOTS*!

Saying thank you is the best way to show someone that you are grateful for them or for something they have done for you. It's a kind thing to do. **When we show people we are thankful for what they have done for us, it makes them feel good and appreciated**. This can make our relationships better and stronger too.

Sometimes we forget to say thank you, but I'd like to encourage you to remember to say it. **Say thank you even for the little things**. For example:

- When your teacher helps you with something
- When somebody cooks you dinner
- When somebody opens a door for you
- When somebody gives you a compliment

Can you think of some kind things people do for you that you will remember to say thank you for next time?

....

....

....

....

....

GRATITUDE CHALLENGE: *Write a letter*

I want you to grab a pen and paper, then write a thank-you letter to somebody special in your life who you are grateful for. Tell them all the reasons you are grateful for them and then give them the letter the next time you see them, or if you know their address you can post it to them. *You will make their day*!

THE BEST PART OF THE DAY

Every night before bed I ask my son, Wolfe, 'What was the best thing about today?' It encourages him to think about all the good things that happened. I'd love you to start doing this every night too. You can do it with a grown-up or write it in a journal.

Let's try it now. In the space below, write down the best things about today.

COMPARING OURSELVES TO OTHER PEOPLE

Sometimes we compare ourselves to other people at school or those we see on TV or on social media. We might see them and decide we aren't as good as them in some way. Or we might feel jealous of those people for the things they have. *Gratitude is about appreciating what we have, but when we compare ourselves to other people it can be harder to do that.*

I remember comparing myself to other girls when I was at school. I would look at the way they dressed, their confidence, how happy they were, and wonder why I wasn't like them. *I wish I could tell my younger self not to feel that way because I was more than good enough exactly as I was!* Have you ever felt like that? If you have, share how this made you feel below.

....

....

....

....

....

....

....

We *all* compare ourselves to others sometimes, and it doesn't feel very nice, does it? **So what can we do next time we notice ourselves doing this?** Well, let me give you a tool you can use to help.

COMPARISON TOOL

1. Remember to appreciate yourself
When we compare ourselves to someone else, we often forget about how special *we* are. We focus on the things that we are not, rather than all the wonderful and amazing things that we already are!

Go back to the answers you wrote down in the 'Celebrating You' exercise in Step Two (see page 75) and read all the things that make you one of a kind! Remember this list and all the brilliant things about you, whenever you start comparing yourself to others.

2. Focus on what you have
When we compare our lives to someone else's, we focus our attention on the things they have, which we don't have, and that makes us feel rubbish! Instead, **focus on what you already have in your life**, by referring back to your list of everything you are grateful for on page 96.

3. Turn jealousy into inspiration
Instead of feeling jealous of someone, you can be inspired by them. Being inspired means that you feel excited or motivated by them. You can use that feeling to help you practise, learn and grow! For example, if you have a friend who gets top

marks in her homework, instead of feeling jealous, you can think, *That's amazing! I want to be able to get top marks too, so I'm going to find a way to make that happen!* You can decide to spend more time on your homework in future, or you can even ask that friend to give you some advice or share some tips that could help you improve.

Being inspired is exciting and it feels so much better than feeling jealous!

<u>I want you to use these tools every time you feel jealous or start comparing yourself to somebody else.</u>

SOCIAL MEDIA

You might already use social media, or you might start to use it soon. It can be very easy to compare ourselves to people on social media, as we are constantly shown all the highlights from other people's lives – the fun they're having, the clothes they're wearing, the holidays they're going on, all the friends they have! This can be really damaging for our confidence. So I want to share this message with you:

Not everything you see online is real.

People can use filters and clever tools that make them look different to how they really are. That means we could be comparing ourselves to people who don't even look like that in real life! People can also make themselves look as though they are *happy all the time* and that *their lives are perfect*. But this isn't true. I promise you that *everyone in the world*, no matter how famous or how successful they are, goes through all the same things that you do. We all feel sad sometimes; we all have times when somebody is unkind to us; and we all have days when we don't feel confident. *And that is what makes us human!*

If being on social media makes you feel good, entertained, inspired or happy, then that's great – that's what it is for! But if it starts to make you feel that you aren't good enough, or you notice that you feel sad after you use it, then here some things you can do:

1. *Delete the apps that make you feel bad* and take a break for a while.
2. *Spend more time with people who make you feel loved* and special.
3. *Say affirmations every day* and keep remembering how amazing you are.
4. *If you go back on the apps, unfollow or mute any accounts that make you feel bad about yourself.* Muting an account means that their content won't come up on your feed any more – you can ask a grown-up to teach you how to do this if you don't know.

FINAL THOUGHTS ON GRATITUDE

To manifest your best life, you need to be thankful for what you already have. When we practise being grateful for what we have, we train our brains to look for and notice more things to be grateful for. Focusing on all the good things in your life will make you feel happier, and it will help you feel more positive during challenging times too.

Life is beautiful and wonderful.
There is always so much
to be grateful for!

STEP FOUR
GOAL-SETTING

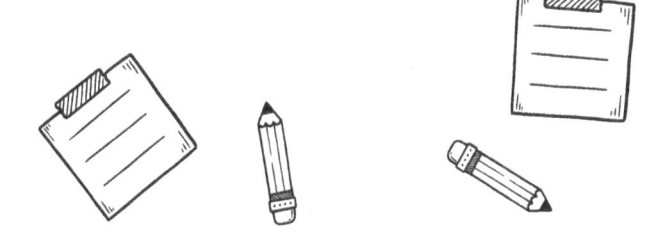

Do you ever think about things that you would like to do in the future? It might be that you want to learn to play guitar or that you want to play netball for your county. Or it could be that you want to make new friends or get better grades in your exams. You might even know what you want to be when you grow up.

All these things are called 'goals'. **Goals are things we want to achieve in the future**. It's important to have goals because it gives us something to focus on, and something to work towards and feel motivated by.

One of the most exciting parts about manifesting is that it helps us reach for our dreams. And you can do this by *goal-setting*.

Here is how to do this:

1. SET YOUR GOALS

The first thing to do is think about what you want to achieve, and when you want to achieve it by. For example:

- Passing your exams by the end of the year
- Joining a sports team by the next school holidays
- Reading a book every month
- Learning ten useful phrases in a different language by the end of term

Let's start this together now. **What are some of your goals for the future?** They can be big, small, far away or soon! Write them down here alongside when you want them to happen by.

....

....

....

....

....

....

....

MAKE A VISION BOARD

A really fun way to become clear on your goals is to make a vision board. Here is how to do it:

- Get a big piece of card or paper and write your name at the top.
- Using coloured pens, stickers, drawings and cut-out images from magazines, put down all the things that represent what you want to achieve. For example, if you want to get the lead part in your school play, you could stick in pictures of theatres and actors who inspire you,

and you could write the name of the play you want to be in and the part you want.
- Stick it up on your wall to remind you of your goals and help keep you focused!

2. VISUALIZE YOUR GOALS

Once you've set goals, imagine them happening in your mind. This is called **visualization**. Visualizing yourself reaching your goals can actually help you to reach them. It's like magic! You need to *picture yourself working towards your goal, overcoming any obstacles and succeeding*. For example, when I wanted to become an author, I pictured myself writing my book, sending it to publishers, and eventually seeing my book on the shelves in shops! It can be hard at first, but with practice, it will become easier.

There are so many famous sportspeople, actors, singers and business owners who have used visualization to help them make their dreams come true. For example, actor, singer and producer Idris Elba OBE said:

> My imagination has always kept me going. I just imagined myself collecting awards. I just imagined myself getting big parts. That's part of my inner magic. If I can see myself doing it, I can do it.

There is also an Olympic swimmer called Michael Phelps who won twenty-eight Olympic medals and twenty-three GOLD

Olympic medals. In fact, he is the most successful Olympian of ALL TIME! He used visualization a lot as part of his training. Before every race, he used to imagine himself swimming, overcoming challenges and winning his races. The visualizations helped him to feel more prepared and more confident, and that helped him win.

> **Our minds are so powerful.**
> We can influence what happens in real life based on what we imagine (or visualize).

Here is how to do a visualization:

1. Lie down on your back and close your eyes.
2. Use your imagination to picture yourself achieving your goals.
3. Visualize as many details as possible. Imagine the colours you can see, the sounds in the scene and how amazing it feels to happen!

When should I do a visualization?

Whenever you have a goal you want achieve or you are nervous about doing something, do a visualization in which you see yourself doing it perfectly. You could do it every night or once a week. The more you visualize it, the better.

3. MAKE A PLAN AND TAKE ACTION

Once we have a goal in mind, we then need to make a plan to help us get there. We can do this **by breaking it down into smaller steps** with lots of *mini goals*. This will help it to feel **more manageable** and **less overwhelming**.

We can also think about what skills we need to practise and how much time we need to spend on it. For example, if our goal is to pass our music exam at the end of the year, we could set ourselves mini goals by deciding which music pieces we need to learn and the order we want to learn them. And we might decide we need to practise for twenty minutes every day to help us reach our goal.

Then we need to **take action**. This means we need to practise and do the work! *Remember, nobody else can do it for us – we have to take responsibility for our own goals.* This sometimes means we have to keep practising or working at something even when it feels hard or like we can't bothered.

This is called self-discipline.

Think of it like this: setting a goal is like planting a seed. For the seed to grow into a beautiful flower, you need to water the plant, give it sunlight and look after it every day. In other words, you have to set the goal (plant the seed) and then continuously *take action* to watch it bloom!

4. BELIEVE IN YOURSELF

In Step Two (see page 71), I talked a lot about the importance of believing in ourselves and building our confidence. *This is very important when we want to reach goals.* If we don't believe in ourselves, we might be afraid to try. If we're too worried about failing, we might never even start! This will obviously make it very hard for us to reach our goals. But if we believe in ourselves, we will be brave enough to go for it even when we feel afraid.

This is a great time to use your affirmations. Keep saying to yourself, 'I can do anything I put my mind to' or 'I can do it!'

If you believe you can, you will!

5. KEEP GOING

Do you ever feel like you want to give up if you get something wrong or make a mistake? It's normal to feel like that sometimes, but to reach our goals we have to stay positive and keep going, even when things aren't going right. *In fact, we have to use our mistakes to help us learn what we can do to get better, grow and go further!*

I promise it's OK if you get something wrong or you can't do it at the start. **The more you try, and the more you practise, the better you will become.** Think about anyone you know who is really talented at something. None of those people started off doing it perfectly. I promise they will have got things wrong and made mistakes too!

> The best thing that we can do when we make a mistake is **to learn from it**. Learning makes us better!

6. LOOK FOR INSPIRATION

When we have big goals we want to reach, we might worry they're impossible. We might even have people in our lives who tell us we can't do something. **But you can do anything you put your mind to.** You are more powerful than you know!

If you know what you want to achieve, it can be very helpful to see or hear about other people who have done it before. This helps us *feel inspired*. Before I started giving big talks to hundreds of people, I used to spend hours watching others doing it. I would listen to them telling their life stories, about how they got to where they are today. It made me feel excited and showed me that I could do it too.

> Read stories or watch videos of people who have accomplished great things and let them show you that it is *more than* possible for you to do great things too.

FINAL THOUGHTS ON GOAL-SETTING

Manifesting helps you to become the person you want to be. Setting and reaching goals is a big part of that. Goals help keep us focused and motivated as we work towards our dreams. And if you don't know what your dreams are yet, that's OK! You have lots of time to try things out and discover what you like. It is so important to keep trying new things. *Trying is a brave thing to do* – you should be so proud of yourself every time you try something you've never done before.

And when you've worked out what your dreams are, use the six steps I shared to help you reach for them. Let me remind you of them here:

1. *Set your goals*
2. *Visualize your goals*
3. *Make a plan and take action*
4. *Believe in yourself*
5. *Keep going*
6. *Look for inspiration*

> Remember that **you can do anything** if you believe in yourself, work hard and **never give up.**

GOAL-SETTING

YOU MADE IT!

I knew you could do it! If you've reached this point, that means you've finished reading this book. Well done, you! You should feel SO proud of yourself. I am proud of you, and I am so grateful that you came on this manifesting journey with me. I want you to live the best life that you can because **you are so special and so wonderfully unique**. You deserve to be happy!

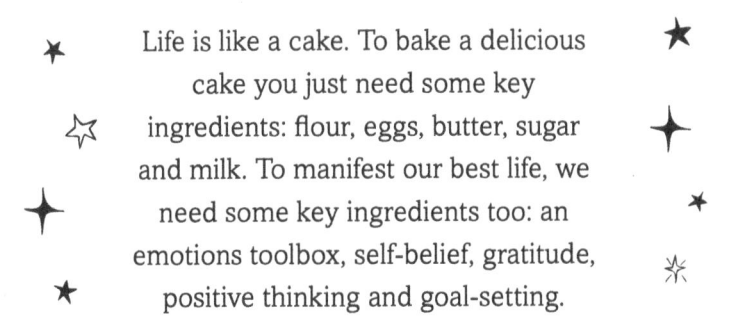

> Life is like a cake. To bake a delicious cake you just need some key ingredients: flour, eggs, butter, sugar and milk. To manifest our best life, we need some key ingredients too: an emotions toolbox, self-belief, gratitude, positive thinking and goal-setting.

This book has given you all the ingredients you need to start manifesting, and to **become the best you** that you can be.

Keep this book somewhere safe and whenever you are having a tough day or you need some extra support, come back and flick through the pages or complete some of the exercises again to help you.

It's now time for you to move on to the second part of this book, which is the daily journal . . . Let's dive in!

PART TWO:
THE JOURNAL

I am so excited for you to start this journal. Writing in my own journal has helped me so much on my manifesting journey, **and I know it will help you too**.

Over the next eight weeks, I want you to fill in this journal every night before you go to bed. It will only take you a few minutes a day, but it will help you to put into practice lots of the things I've taught you in this book. If you miss a day, don't worry, but try to complete as many days as you can.

On the next page is an example of how to fill in the journal, and then you can start yours.

What emotions did you feel today?

Worry

Happiness

Pride

What were the best things that happened today?

It was sports day at school, and we stopped at the ice cream van afterwards.

What were you proud of yourself for doing today?

It was sports day and even though I was worried about not doing well in front of everyone, I tried really hard in my running race and came third!

Did you use any tools from your emotions toolbox to help you? If so, which did you use and how did they help?

I used 'change the channel' to stop worrying.

What are you excited about for tomorrow?

It's the weekend and we're going to go to the cinema.

Say this affirmation to yourself five times:

I am loved just the way I am.

's Journal

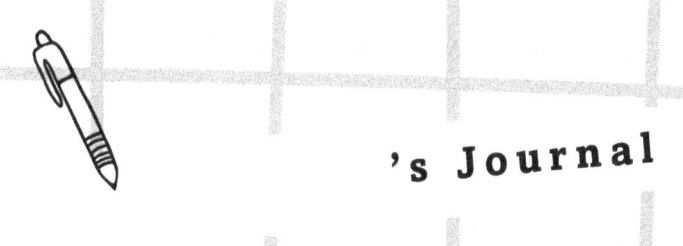

Date started:

MONDAY

What emotions did you feel today?

....
....
....

What were the best things that happened today?

....
....
....
....
....
....

What were you proud of yourself for doing today?

....
....
....
....
....
....
....

WEEK 1

Did you use any tools from your emotions toolbox to help you? If so, which did you use and how did they help?

....
....
....
....
....
....
....

What are you excited about for tomorrow?

....
....
....
....
....
....

Say this affirmation to yourself five times.

I am loved just the way I am.

TUESDAY

What emotions did you feel today?

....

....

....

What were the best things that happened today?

....

....

....

....

....

....

What were you proud of yourself for doing today?

....

....

....

....

....

....

....

WEEK 1

Did you use any tools from your emotions toolbox to help you? If so, which did you use and how did they help?

....
....
....
....
....
....
....
....

What are you excited about for tomorrow?

....
....
....
....
....
....

Say this affirmation to yourself five times.

I am strong.

WEDNESDAY

What emotions did you feel today?

....

....

....

What were the best things that happened today?

....

....

....

....

....

....

What were you proud of yourself for doing today?

....

....

....

....

....

....

WEEK 1

Did you use any tools from your emotions toolbox to help you? If so, which did you use and how did they help?

....
....
....
....
....
....
....
....

What are you excited about for tomorrow?

....
....
....
....
....

Say this affirmation to yourself five times.

I believe in myself.

THURSDAY

What emotions did you feel today?

....

....

....

What were the best things that happened today?

....

....

....

....

....

....

What were you proud of yourself for doing today?

....

....

....

....

....

....

Did you use any tools from your emotions toolbox to help you? If so, which did you use and how did they help?

....
....
....
....
....
....
....

What are you excited about for tomorrow?

....
....
....
....
....
....

Say this affirmation to yourself five times.

I can be anybody I want to be.

FRIDAY

What emotions did you feel today?

....

....

....

What were the best things that happened today?

....

....

....

....

....

....

What were you proud of yourself for doing today?

....

....

....

....

....

....

WEEK 1

Did you use any tools from your emotions toolbox to help you? If so, which did you use and how did they help?

....

....

....

....

....

....

....

What are you excited about for tomorrow?

....

....

....

....

....

....

Say this affirmation to yourself five times.

I am proud of myself.

SATURDAY

What emotions did you feel today?

....

....

....

What were the best things that happened today?

....

....

....

....

....

....

What were you proud of yourself for doing today?

....

....

....

....

....

....

....

WEEK 1

Did you use any tools from your emotions toolbox to help you? If so, which did you use and how did they help?

....

....

....

....

....

....

....

What are you excited about for tomorrow?

....

....

....

....

....

....

Say this affirmation to yourself five times.

I deserve to be happy.

SUNDAY

What emotions did you feel today?

....

....

....

What were the best things that happened today?

....

....

....

....

....

....

What were you proud of yourself for doing today?

....

....

....

....

....

....

....

Did you use any tools from your emotions toolbox to help you? If so, which did you use and how did they help?

....
....
....
....
....
....
....
....

What are you excited about for tomorrow?

....
....
....
....
....
....

Say this affirmation to yourself five times.

I get better every day.

MONDAY

What emotions did you feel today?

....

....

....

What were the best things that happened today?

....

....

....

....

....

....

What were you proud of yourself for doing today?

....

....

....

....

....

....

WEEK 2

Did you use any tools from your emotions toolbox to help you? If so, which did you use and how did they help?

....
....
....
....
....
....
....

What are you excited about for tomorrow?

....
....
....
....
....
....

Say this affirmation to yourself five times.

I can do anything I put my mind to.

TUESDAY

What emotions did you feel today?

....
....
....

What were the best things that happened today?

....
....
....
....
....
....

What were you proud of yourself for doing today?

....
....
....
....
....
....

WEEK 2

Did you use any tools from your emotions toolbox to help you? If so, which did you use and how did they help?

....
....
....
....
....
....
....
....

What are you excited about for tomorrow?

....
....
....
....
....
....

Say this affirmation to yourself five times.

I can overcome any obstacle.

WEDNESDAY

What emotions did you feel today?

....

....

....

What were the best things that happened today?

....

....

....

....

....

....

What were you proud of yourself for doing today?

....

....

....

....

....

....

WEEK 2

Did you use any tools from your emotions toolbox to help you? If so, which did you use and how did they help?

....
....
....
....
....
....
....

What are you excited about for tomorrow?

....
....
....
....
....
....

Say this affirmation to yourself five times.

I am excited for the future.

THURSDAY

What emotions did you feel today?

....
....
....

What were the best things that happened today?

....
....
....
....
....
....

What were you proud of yourself for doing today?

....
....
....
....
....
....
....

WEEK 2

Did you use any tools from your emotions toolbox to help you? If so, which did you use and how did they help?

....
....
....
....
....
....
....
....

What are you excited about for tomorrow?

....
....
....
....
....
....

Say this affirmation to yourself five times.

I am enough.

FRIDAY

What emotions did you feel today?

....

....

....

What were the best things that happened today?

....

....

....

....

....

....

What were you proud of yourself for doing today?

....

....

....

....

....

....

....

WEEK 2

Did you use any tools from your emotions toolbox to help you? If so, which did you use and how did they help?

....
....
....
....
....
....
....
....

What are you excited about for tomorrow?

....
....
....
....
....
....

Say this affirmation to yourself five times.

I believe in myself.

SATURDAY

What emotions did you feel today?

....

....

....

What were the best things that happened today?

....

....

....

....

....

....

What were you proud of yourself for doing today?

....

....

....

....

....

....

....

WEEK 2

Did you use any tools from your emotions toolbox to help you? If so, which did you use and how did they help?

....
....
....
....
....
....
....
....

What are you excited about for tomorrow?

....
....
....
....
....
....

Say this affirmation to yourself five times.

I am brave and courageous.

SUNDAY

What emotions did you feel today?

....

....

....

What were the best things that happened today?

....

....

....

....

....

....

What were you proud of yourself for doing today?

....

....

....

....

....

....

....

WEEK 2

Did you use any tools from your emotions toolbox to help you? If so, which did you use and how did they help?

....
....
....
....
....
....
....
....

What are you excited about for tomorrow?

....
....
....
....
....
....

Say this affirmation to yourself five times.

I am special and unique.

MONDAY

What emotions did you feel today?

....
....
....

What were the best things that happened today?

....
....
....
....
....
....

What were you proud of yourself for doing today?

....
....
....
....
....
....
....

WEEK 3

Did you use any tools from your emotions toolbox to help you? If so, which did you use and how did they help?

....
....
....
....
....
....
....
....

What are you excited about for tomorrow?

....
....
....
....
....
....

Say this affirmation to yourself five times.

Today is going to be an amazing day.

TUESDAY

What emotions did you feel today?

....

....

....

What were the best things that happened today?

....

....

....

....

....

....

What were you proud of yourself for doing today?

....

....

....

....

....

....

Did you use any tools from your emotions toolbox to help you? If so, which did you use and how did they help?

....
....
....
....
....
....
....
....

What are you excited about for tomorrow?

....
....
....
....
....
....

Say this affirmation to yourself five times.

I am always learning and growing.

WEEK 3

WEDNESDAY

What emotions did you feel today?

....

....

....

What were the best things that happened today?

....

....

....

....

....

....

What were you proud of yourself for doing today?

....

....

....

....

....

....

....

WEEK 3

Did you use any tools from your emotions toolbox to help you? If so, which did you use and how did they help?

....
....
....
....
....
....
....

What are you excited about for tomorrow?

....
....
....
....
....
....

Say this affirmation to yourself five times.

I can get through anything.

THURSDAY

What emotions did you feel today?

....
....
....

What were the best things that happened today?

....
....
....
....
....
....

What were you proud of yourself for doing today?

....
....
....
....
....
....
....

WEEK 3

Did you use any tools from your emotions toolbox to help you? If so, which did you use and how did they help?

....
....
....
....
....
....
....

What are you excited about for tomorrow?

....
....
....
....
....
....

Say this affirmation to yourself five times.

I matter to the people in my life.

FRIDAY

What emotions did you feel today?

....

....

....

What were the best things that happened today?

....

....

....

....

....

....

What were you proud of yourself for doing today?

....

....

....

....

....

....

WEEK 3

Did you use any tools from your emotions toolbox to help you? If so, which did you use and how did they help?

....
....
....
....
....
....
....
....

What are you excited about for tomorrow?

....
....
....
....
....
....

Say this affirmation to yourself five times.

I am a good person.

SATURDAY

What emotions did you feel today?

....

....

....

What were the best things that happened today?

....

....

....

....

....

What were you proud of yourself for doing today?

....

....

....

....

....

....

WEEK 3

Did you use any tools from your emotions toolbox to help you? If so, which did you use and how did they help?

....
....
....
....
....
....
....
....

What are you excited about for tomorrow?

....
....
....
....
....
....

Say this affirmation to yourself five times.

I can and I will.

SUNDAY

What emotions did you feel today?

....

....

....

What were the best things that happened today?

....

....

....

....

....

....

What were you proud of yourself for doing today?

....

....

....

....

....

....

WEEK 3

Did you use any tools from your emotions toolbox to help you? If so, which did you use and how did they help?

....
....
....
....
....
....
....

What are you excited about for tomorrow?

....
....
....
....
....
....

Say this affirmation to yourself five times.

It is enough to do my best.

MONDAY

What emotions did you feel today?

....

....

....

What were the best things that happened today?

....

....

....

....

....

....

What were you proud of yourself for doing today?

....

....

....

....

....

....

....

WEEK 4

Did you use any tools from your emotions toolbox to help you? If so, which did you use and how did they help?

....
....
....
....
....
....
....
....

What are you excited about for tomorrow?

....
....
....
....
....
....

Say this affirmation to yourself five times.

I am worthy of love and happiness.

TUESDAY

What emotions did you feel today?

....
....
....

What were the best things that happened today?

....
....
....
....
....
....

What were you proud of yourself for doing today?

....
....
....
....
....
....
....

WEEK 4

Did you use any tools from your emotions toolbox to help you? If so, which did you use and how did they help?

....
....
....
....
....
....
....
....

What are you excited about for tomorrow?

....
....
....
....
....
....

Say this affirmation to yourself five times.

I am important to the world.

WEDNESDAY

What emotions did you feel today?

....

....

....

What were the best things that happened today?

....

....

....

....

....

....

What were you proud of yourself for doing today?

....

....

....

....

....

....

....

WEEK 4

Did you use any tools from your emotions toolbox to help you? If so, which did you use and how did they help?

....
....
....
....
....
....
....
....

What are you excited about for tomorrow?

....
....
....
....
....
....

Say this affirmation to yourself five times.

Challenges help me grow.

THURSDAY

What emotions did you feel today?

....
....
....

What were the best things that happened today?

....
....
....
....
....
....

What were you proud of yourself for doing today?

....
....
....
....
....
....

WEEK 4

Did you use any tools from your emotions toolbox to help you? If so, which did you use and how did they help?

....
....
....
....
....
....
....
....

What are you excited about for tomorrow?

....
....
....
....
....
....

Say this affirmation to yourself five times.

I am amazing.

FRIDAY

What emotions did you feel today?

....

....

....

What were the best things that happened today?

....

....

....

....

....

....

What were you proud of yourself for doing today?

....

....

....

....

....

....

....

WEEK 4

Did you use any tools from your emotions toolbox to help you? If so, which did you use and how did they help?

....
....
....
....
....
....
....
....

What are you excited about for tomorrow?

....
....
....
....
....
....

Say this affirmation to yourself five times.

I am loved just the way I am.

SATURDAY

What emotions did you feel today?

....

....

....

What were the best things that happened today?

....

....

....

....

....

....

What were you proud of yourself for doing today?

....

....

....

....

....

....

....

WEEK 4

Did you use any tools from your emotions toolbox to help you? If so, which did you use and how did they help?

....

....

....

....

....

....

....

....

What are you excited about for tomorrow?

....

....

....

....

....

....

Say this affirmation to yourself five times.

I am strong.

SUNDAY

What emotions did you feel today?

....

....

....

What were the best things that happened today?

....

....

....

....

....

....

What were you proud of yourself for doing today?

....

....

....

....

....

....

....

WEEK 4

Did you use any tools from your emotions toolbox to help you? If so, which did you use and how did they help?

....
....
....
....
....
....
....
....

What are you excited about for tomorrow?

....
....
....
....
....
....

Say this affirmation to yourself five times.

I believe in myself.

MONDAY

What emotions did you feel today?

....

....

....

What were the best things that happened today?

....

....

....

....

....

....

What were you proud of yourself for doing today?

....

....

....

....

....

....

WEEK 5

Did you use any tools from your emotions toolbox to help you? If so, which did you use and how did they help?

....
....
....
....
....
....
....
....

What are you excited about for tomorrow?

....
....
....
....
....
....

Say this affirmation to yourself five times.

I can be anybody I want to be.

TUESDAY

What emotions did you feel today?

....

....

....

What were the best things that happened today?

....

....

....

....

....

....

What were you proud of yourself for doing today?

....

....

....

....

....

....

WEEK 5

Did you use any tools from your emotions toolbox to help you? If so, which did you use and how did they help?

....

....

....

....

....

....

....

What are you excited about for tomorrow?

....

....

....

....

....

....

Say this affirmation to yourself five times.

I am proud of myself.

WEDNESDAY

What emotions did you feel today?

....

....

....

What were the best things that happened today?

....

....

....

....

....

....

What were you proud of yourself for doing today?

....

....

....

....

....

....

WEEK 5

Did you use any tools from your emotions toolbox to help you? If so, which did you use and how did they help?

....
....
....
....
....
....
....
....

What are you excited about for tomorrow?

....
....
....
....
....
....

Say this affirmation to yourself five times.

I deserve to be happy.

THURSDAY

What emotions did you feel today?

....
....
....

What were the best things that happened today?

....
....
....
....
....
....

What were you proud of yourself for doing today?

....
....
....
....
....
....

WEEK 5

Did you use any tools from your emotions toolbox to help you? If so, which did you use and how did they help?

....
....
....
....
....
....
....
....

What are you excited about for tomorrow?

....
....
....
....
....
....

Say this affirmation to yourself five times.

I get better every day.

FRIDAY

What emotions did you feel today?

....

....

....

What were the best things that happened today?

....

....

....

....

....

....

What were you proud of yourself for doing today?

....

....

....

....

....

....

WEEK 5

Did you use any tools from your emotions toolbox to help you? If so, which did you use and how did they help?

....
....
....
....
....
....
....
....

What are you excited about for tomorrow?

....
....
....
....
....
....

Say this affirmation to yourself five times.

I can do anything I put my mind to.

SATURDAY

What emotions did you feel today?

....

....

....

What were the best things that happened today?

....

....

....

....

....

....

What were you proud of yourself for doing today?

....

....

....

....

....

....

....

WEEK 5

Did you use any tools from your emotions toolbox to help you? If so, which did you use and how did they help?

....
....
....
....
....
....
....
....

What are you excited about for tomorrow?

....
....
....
....
....
....

Say this affirmation to yourself five times.

I can overcome any obstacle.

SUNDAY

What emotions did you feel today?

....

....

....

What were the best things that happened today?

....

....

....

....

....

....

What were you proud of yourself for doing today?

....

....

....

....

....

....

....

WEEK 5

Did you use any tools from your emotions toolbox to help you? If so, which did you use and how did they help?

....

....

....

....

....

....

....

....

What are you excited about for tomorrow?

....

....

....

....

....

....

Say this affirmation to yourself five times.

I am excited for the future.

MONDAY

What emotions did you feel today?

....

....

....

What were the best things that happened today?

....

....

....

....

....

....

What were you proud of yourself for doing today?

....

....

....

....

....

....

....

WEEK 6

Did you use any tools from your emotions toolbox to help you? If so, which did you use and how did they help?

....

....

....

....

....

....

....

What are you excited about for tomorrow?

....

....

....

....

....

....

Say this affirmation to yourself five times.

I am enough.

TUESDAY

What emotions did you feel today?

....

....

....

What were the best things that happened today?

....

....

....

....

....

....

What were you proud of yourself for doing today?

....

....

....

....

....

....

WEEK 6

Did you use any tools from your emotions toolbox to help you? If so, which did you use and how did they help?

....

....

....

....

....

....

....

What are you excited about for tomorrow?

....

....

....

....

....

....

Say this affirmation to yourself five times.

I believe in myself.

WEDNESDAY

What emotions did you feel today?

....

....

....

What were the best things that happened today?

....

....

....

....

....

....

What were you proud of yourself for doing today?

....

....

....

....

....

....

....

WEEK 6

Did you use any tools from your emotions toolbox to help you? If so, which did you use and how did they help?

....
....
....
....
....
....
....

What are you excited about for tomorrow?

....
....
....
....
....
....

Say this affirmation to yourself five times.

I am brave and courageous.

THURSDAY

What emotions did you feel today?

....
....
....

What were the best things that happened today?

....
....
....
....
....
....

What were you proud of yourself for doing today?

....
....
....
....
....
....

WEEK 6

Did you use any tools from your emotions toolbox to help you? If so, which did you use and how did they help?

....
....
....
....
....
....
....
....

What are you excited about for tomorrow?

....
....
....
....
....
....

Say this affirmation to yourself five times.

I am special and unique.

FRIDAY

What emotions did you feel today?

....

....

....

What were the best things that happened today?

....

....

....

....

....

....

What were you proud of yourself for doing today?

....

....

....

....

....

....

....

WEEK 6

Did you use any tools from your emotions toolbox to help you? If so, which did you use and how did they help?

....
....
....
....
....
....
....
....

What are you excited about for tomorrow?

....
....
....
....
....
....

Say this affirmation to yourself five times.

Today is going to be an amazing day.

SATURDAY

What emotions did you feel today?

....

....

....

What were the best things that happened today?

....

....

....

....

....

....

What were you proud of yourself for doing today?

....

....

....

....

....

....

WEEK 6

Did you use any tools from your emotions toolbox to help you? If so, which did you use and how did they help?

....
....
....
....
....
....
....
....

What are you excited about for tomorrow?

....
....
....
....
....
....

Say this affirmation to yourself five times.

I am always learning and growing.

SUNDAY

What emotions did you feel today?

....

....

....

What were the best things that happened today?

....

....

....

....

....

....

What were you proud of yourself for doing today?

....

....

....

....

....

....

WEEK 6

Did you use any tools from your emotions toolbox to help you? If so, which did you use and how did they help?

....
....
....
....
....
....
....
....

What are you excited about for tomorrow?

....
....
....
....
....
....

Say this affirmation to yourself five times.

I can get through anything.

MONDAY

What emotions did you feel today?

....
....
....

What were the best things that happened today?

....
....
....
....
....
....

What were you proud of yourself for doing today?

....
....
....
....
....
....

WEEK 7

Did you use any tools from your emotions toolbox to help you? If so, which did you use and how did they help?

....
....
....
....
....
....
....
....

What are you excited about for tomorrow?

....
....
....
....
....
....

Say this affirmation to yourself five times.

I matter to the people in my life.

TUESDAY

What emotions did you feel today?

....

....

....

What were the best things that happened today?

....

....

....

....

....

....

What were you proud of yourself for doing today?

....

....

....

....

....

....

WEEK 7

Did you use any tools from your emotions toolbox to help you? If so, which did you use and how did they help?

....
....
....
....
....
....
....
....

What are you excited about for tomorrow?

....
....
....
....
....
....

Say this affirmation to yourself five times.

I am a good person.

WEDNESDAY

What emotions did you feel today?

....

....

....

What were the best things that happened today?

....

....

....

....

....

....

What were you proud of yourself for doing today?

....

....

....

....

....

....

WEEK 7

Did you use any tools from your emotions toolbox to help you? If so, which did you use and how did they help?

....
....
....
....
....
....
....
....

What are you excited about for tomorrow?

....
....
....
....
....
....

Say this affirmation to yourself five times.

I can and I will.

THURSDAY

What emotions did you feel today?

....

....

....

What were the best things that happened today?

....

....

....

....

....

....

What were you proud of yourself for doing today?

....

....

....

....

....

....

WEEK 7

Did you use any tools from your emotions toolbox to help you? If so, which did you use and how did they help?

....
....
....
....
....
....
....

What are you excited about for tomorrow?

....
....
....
....
....
....

Say this affirmation to yourself five times.

It is enough to do my best.

FRIDAY

What emotions did you feel today?

....
....
....

What were the best things that happened today?

....
....
....
....
....
....

What were you proud of yourself for doing today?

....
....
....
....
....
....
....

WEEK 7

Did you use any tools from your emotions toolbox to help you? If so, which did you use and how did they help?

....
....
....
....
....
....
....
....

What are you excited about for tomorrow?

....
....
....
....
....
....

Say this affirmation to yourself five times.

I am worthy of love and happiness.

SATURDAY

What emotions did you feel today?

....

....

....

What were the best things that happened today?

....

....

....

....

....

....

What were you proud of yourself for doing today?

....

....

....

....

....

....

....

WEEK 7

Did you use any tools from your emotions toolbox to help you? If so, which did you use and how did they help?

....
....
....
....
....
....
....
....

What are you excited about for tomorrow?

....
....
....
....
....
....

Say this affirmation to yourself five times.

I am important to the world.

SUNDAY

What emotions did you feel today?

....

....

....

What were the best things that happened today?

....

....

....

....

....

....

What were you proud of yourself for doing today?

....

....

....

....

....

....

....

Did you use any tools from your emotions toolbox to help you? If so, which did you use and how did they help?

....
....
....
....
....
....
....
....

What are you excited about for tomorrow?

....
....
....
....
....
....

Say this affirmation to yourself five times.

Challenges help me grow.

WEEK 7

MONDAY

What emotions did you feel today?

....

....

....

What were the best things that happened today?

....

....

....

....

....

....

What were you proud of yourself for doing today?

....

....

....

....

....

....

WEEK 8

Did you use any tools from your emotions toolbox to help you? If so, which did you use and how did they help?

....
....
....
....
....
....
....

What are you excited about for tomorrow?

....
....
....
....
....
....

Say this affirmation to yourself five times.

I am amazing.

TUESDAY

What emotions did you feel today?

....

....

....

What were the best things that happened today?

....

....

....

....

....

....

What were you proud of yourself for doing today?

....

....

....

....

....

....

....

WEEK 8

Did you use any tools from your emotions toolbox to help you? If so, which did you use and how did they help?

....
....
....
....
....
....
....
....

What are you excited about for tomorrow?

....
....
....
....
....
....

Say this affirmation to yourself five times.

I am always learning and growing.

WEDNESDAY

What emotions did you feel today?

....
....
....

What were the best things that happened today?

....
....
....
....
....
....

What were you proud of yourself for doing today?

....
....
....
....
....
....
....

WEEK 8

Did you use any tools from your emotions toolbox to help you? If so, which did you use and how did they help?

....
....
....
....
....
....
....

What are you excited about for tomorrow?

....
....
....
....
....
....

Say this affirmation to yourself five times.

I deserve to be happy.

THURSDAY

What emotions did you feel today?

....

....

....

What were the best things that happened today?

....

....

....

....

....

What were you proud of yourself for doing today?

....

....

....

....

....

....

WEEK 8

Did you use any tools from your emotions toolbox to help you? If so, which did you use and how did they help?

....
....
....
....
....
....
....
....

What are you excited about for tomorrow?

....
....
....
....
....
....

Say this affirmation to yourself five times.

I am brave and courageous.

FRIDAY

What emotions did you feel today?

....

....

....

What were the best things that happened today?

....

....

....

....

....

....

What were you proud of yourself for doing today?

....

....

....

....

....

....

WEEK 8

Did you use any tools from your emotions toolbox to help you? If so, which did you use and how did they help?

....

....

....

....

....

....

....

What are you excited about for tomorrow?

....

....

....

....

....

....

Say this affirmation to yourself five times.

I matter to the people in my life.

SATURDAY

What emotions did you feel today?

....
....
....

What were the best things that happened today?

....
....
....
....
....
....

What were you proud of yourself for doing today?

....
....
....
....
....
....
....

WEEK 8

Did you use any tools from your emotions toolbox to help you? If so, which did you use and how did they help?

....
....
....
....
....
....
....
....

What are you excited about for tomorrow?

....
....
....
....
....
....

Say this affirmation to yourself five times.

Today is going to be an amazing day.

SUNDAY

What emotions did you feel today?

....

....

....

What were the best things that happened today?

....

....

....

....

....

....

What were you proud of yourself for doing today?

....

....

....

....

....

....

WEEK 8

Did you use any tools from your emotions toolbox to help you? If so, which did you use and how did they help?

....
....
....
....
....
....
....
....

What are you excited about for tomorrow?

....
....
....
....
....
....

Say this affirmation to yourself five times.

I am loved just the way I am.

A NOTE FOR THE GROWN-UPS

Hello Grown-Up,

Firstly, thank you so much for helping to get this book into the reader's hands! Whether you have it at home or you are a teacher working through it with your class, I want to explain a little bit about why I wrote this book and what I hope it will achieve. Then I want to share how I think you can best support the person who is reading it.

Manifestation is a practice that has changed my life beyond recognition. I discovered it back in 2018 when my life was *completely different*. I was extremely lost, with no self-worth, prospects or hope for the future. I completely immersed myself in learning as much as I could on the subject of manifesting and then broke it down into seven practical steps. As I followed these steps myself, I saw every area of my life change for the better. I finally found happiness, confidence and self-love after decades without it.

Manifesting is a self-development practice to live by. It's not about manifesting 'things' into our life; *although that is a wonderful bonus*, it is about becoming the best version of ourselves that we can be. It is about becoming so empowered and so full of self-belief that *we make things happen*. We dare to dream and we keep going even when we are faced with challenges or obstacles. *We take action to make sure that we are living a life that makes us content, fulfilled and happy.*

I have been honoured to teach many adults about this incredible practice, and now I am excited to be sharing it with young people. Our childhood and early teen years are so integral to who we become, and I know first-hand how challenging those years can be. I want to help as many children as I can to **realize their potential, build resilience, know their worth and be proud to be themselves**.

The four steps to manifesting that I have created for children are aimed at helping them build the strong foundations that I believe they need *to live their best lives*. I hope that everybody who reads this book will use the tools they've learned to help them live better day to day and feel more equipped to cope with the everyday struggles that growing up in the modern world brings. But for the benefits of this book to be seen and felt, it is also going to need YOUR help!

Young people are hugely influenced and affected by the trusted adults in their lives, and we all have a responsibility to ensure children have their basic needs met. Some of these basic needs are to **feel safe, loved, heard, seen and validated**. When these needs are met, and we support children as they work through the tools in this book, we can have a profoundly positive impact on their self-esteem and overall well-being.

On the next pages I will share why I believe each step is so important to children's manifesting process, and then give some advice on practical ways to support children as they work through each step.

1. UNDERSTANDING OUR EMOTIONS

Emotions are all energy; they hold weight, and when they are not understood or processed they get stuck within our body. If we don't know how to cope with our sadness, anger or guilt, it gets locked into us and then comes out in other ways throughout life. **Trapped emotions can manifest as anxiety, low self-worth and depression.**

Knowing how to safely let out, understand and cope with our emotions is key. Most children don't have the tools they need to do this; *in fact, most grown-ups don't!* As children, many of us *learned to avoid, hide or judge our 'negative' emotions, and so now we are well rehearsed at avoiding them as adults.* I created an emotions toolbox to help the readers of this book validate their emotions (by saying them out loud and to somebody else) and find ways to cope with them and let them out so that they don't build up and overwhelm them.

How to support this

As I am trying to encourage children to be open about how they are feeling, it is important that you support this by *providing a safe space* for them to do so.

Safety is an integral part of a child's development, but this doesn't just mean physical safety. Emotional safety means that your child is able to express the full spectrum of emotions without being condemned, scolded or judged for it. For example, rather than punishing your child for crying, or shouting at them for being angry, try to create space for them to express themselves while encouraging and helping them use the tools I've suggested. Remember that *all emotions are valid.*

> *Try this:*
> *Create a set time each day where the reader can come and talk to you and express everything they've been feeling and thinking. Be there to listen, without any judgement. This is a simple way to start to introduce a safe, open space that will help them feel more able to come to you.*

2. CONFIDENCE AND SELF-BELIEF

The biggest secret of manifesting is this: *we manifest what we subconsciously believe we are worthy of receiving.* We cannot manifest our best life, or become the best versions of ourselves, if we don't believe in ourselves. Self-belief and self-worth are built over time, and the earlier we can learn to love and appreciate who we are, the more empowered we will become. From about the age of eight, social pressures begin: we can start to feel that we don't fit in with our peers or we start to see our differences as reasons to believe we aren't good enough as we are. So it is *absolutely integral* that we support the self-esteem of young people during this time: to show them that their differences are things to be proud of.

The aim of this book is to help young people see how special they are, to find ways to be kinder to themselves and to learn tools that they can use throughout their lives to help them believe they are worthy of abundance, love and joy. All the tools I teach in this book are tools that I use every day, *so perhaps let the reader teach them to you too*!

How to support this

The best thing you can do is encourage them. Encourage the reader to celebrate their uniqueness and think about what they felt proud of each day, no matter how small. Encourage the use of positive affirmations, especially in times of self-doubt. Encourage them to keep going when things get tough and encourage them to speak kindly to themselves.

Also, remember that children *are always learning from us*. How you treat yourself matters to them. Be kind to yourself, speak to yourself *and about yourself* in a self-loving manner, and commit to your own well-being practices too! **If you show yourself love, kindness and respect, that's what the child in your life will learn and imitate.**

I also think it's important that we are conscious of not trying to indirectly mould children into who we want them to be, but instead allow them to grow into the person that they truly are.

3. GRATITUDE

There is wide-reaching scientific research that shows the positive impact gratitude has on our well-being, both physical and mental. If we can encourage children to develop a more grateful attitude by practising gratitude regularly, we will help them feel happier, improve their mental health and even strengthen their immune systems!

I believe that the best thing you can do is to *model gratitude*, so be mindful of what you say around them. Are you often complaining about things or expressing your own stress or anger? If so, can you try instead to express more thanks and appreciation? Not only will this help them, but it will help you to feel better too. Also, make an effort to say 'thank you' to them more for the little things that they do, just as I have encouraged them to do with others.

> *Try this:*
> *If you hear your child complaining or moaning, gently encourage them to find something positive to say afterwards. For example, if they say, 'I hate this place,' you could say, 'I understand that's how you're feeling right now. But is there one positive thing you could say about it?' If they can't think of anything, you could share a few things you can think of. With this approach, you're not dismissing their feelings but helping them to search for the good in any situation.*

4. GOAL-SETTING

A big benefit of manifesting is that it helps us to set and reach goals. It helps us to attract abundance into our lives, and to turn our dreams into reality. I wanted to introduce this concept to young people by helping them get into the practice of going for the things they want and seeing for themselves how much limitless potential lies within them.

How to support this

To aid young people in this step, encourage them to try to believe in themselves, and to keep going even when it gets hard. Perhaps you could share examples of when you have persisted through challenges or share inspirational stories about people who have achieved great things. Remind them that they can do great things too.

If you haven't read my book for grown-ups – *MANIFEST: 7 Steps to Living Your Best Life* – now could be a great time, so that you can lead by example as you unlock YOUR best self!

We all want the best for the children in our lives. I hate the thought of my son having the same crippling self-loathing that I lived with. In fact, I hate the thought of any child living that way. It's not easy being a young person, especially in the age of social media and the internet; it's more important than ever to help equip children with tools that can help them become more confident, more resilient and more aware of their own emotional processes.

> If we can help children learn to manifest and become their best selves, **we have the power** to change a generation.

Thank you, from the bottom of my heart, for supporting my mission!

RESOURCES

If you want to learn more about anything covered in this book or if you need advice from experts, here are some organizations that can help:

CHILDLINE
A free and private service for anyone under the age of nineteen. They have a 24-hour helpline that you can call for free on 0800 1111 if you want to talk to a counsellor, and there is lots of helpful information on their website too.
https://www.childline.org.uk/

HEALTH FOR KIDS
This NHS website has lots of games, activities and information to help you understand your feelings and how you can look after your mind and body.
https://www.healthforkids.co.uk/

HUB OF HOPE
A database to help you find support that is right for you.
https://hubofhope.co.uk/

MINDFULNESS ACTIVITIES FOR KIDS
32 mindfulness activities for children, teenagers and adults that can help you to relieve stress and be more present in the moment.
https://www.healthline.com/health/mind-body/mindfulness-activities

SAMARITANS
An organization that is available 24 hours a day, 365 days a year to provide support. You can call them for free on 116 123. They also have a self-help app on their website.
https://www.samaritans.org/

SHOUT
A free, confidential 24-hour support service for anyone in the UK who is struggling to cope. You text the word SHOUT to 85258 and a trained volunteer will be there to listen and help.

YOUNGMINDS
A mental health charity that offers advice to children and teenagers on how to feel better or support someone else who is struggling.
https://youngminds.org.uk

YOU WILL BE OKAY by Julie Stokes
A comforting and practical book and toolkit for children age 9+ dealing with loss and grief, by chartered clinical psychologist Julie Stokes OBE.